They Played Baseball for the Yankees?

A History of Forgotten Bronx Bombers

By Jeff Wagner

They Played Baseball for the Yankees?

Copyright © 2020 Jeff Wagner

ISBN: 978-1-61170-295-8

All rights reserved. No part of this publication may be reproduced, stored in a retrieval system or transmitted in any form or by any means, electronic, mechanical, photocopies, recording or otherwise, without the prior written consent of the publisher, except in the case of brief quotations embodied in critical reviews.

Published by:

Robertson Publishing™
www.RobertsonPublishing.com

Printed in the USA and UK on acid-free paper.

Dedication

This book is dedicated to the memory of my father, Jim Wagner, who took me to my first professional basketball game in 1966, my first professional hockey game in 1969, my first professional baseball game in 1971, and my first professional football game in 1975. He not only introduced me to the world of sports, but instilled the importance of good sportsmanship and team work whenever playing one.

Also to the memory of my sister Julie Martinez, who was probably a bigger local sports fan than I was!

I would like to thank Jan for her extra pair of eyes.

And last but not least, I would also like to thank my loving wife Amy for her support, even though she has little to no interest in baseball. Thanks for the encouragement!

Table of Contents

Introduction	1
The Start of Something Big	3
Hal Chase	4
Bobby Cox	5
Dazzy Vance	6
Deion Sanders	7
George Halas	8
J.T. Snow	9
Jackie Jensen	10
Lefty O'Doul	11
Leo Durocher	12
Lew Burdette	13
Hello and Goodbye	14
Bobby Bonds	15
Branch Rickey	16
Carl Mays	17
Cecil Fielder	18
Clark Griffith	19
Enos Slaughter	20
Felipe Alou	21
Gaylord Perry	22
Ivan Rodriquez	23
Jack Clark	24
Joe Niekro	25
John Candelaria	26
Johnny Sain	27
Jose Canseco	28
Ken Griffey, Sr.	29
Lee Smith	30
Luis Tiant	31
Matty Alou	32
Pete Incaviglia	33
Phil Niekro	34
Randy Johnson	35
Sal Maglie	36
Sam McDowell	37
Tim Raines	38
Toby Harrah	39
The End of the Line	40
Bert Campaneris	41
Darryl Strawberry	42
Dwight Gooden	43

Frank Chance	44
Home Run Baker	45
Jeff Reardon	46
John Mayberry	47
Johnny Mize	48
Kevin Brown	49
Paul Waner	50
Other Players of Note	51
The Yankees by the Numbers	52
The Yankees – a Timeline	54
Book Sources	63
Author's Bio	64

Introduction

The Yankees have had a large and storied role in the history of Major League Baseball. Going back to its roots in New York as the Highlanders in 1903, the "Bronx Bombers" are arguably the most successful franchise in Major League Baseball history, having made the most visits to the post season (55), while winning more pennants (40) and World Series titles (27) than any other team. Their .570 winning percentage is tops in baseball history.

THE YANKEES IN HISTORY

TEAM NAMES:	Highlanders, Yankees
SEASONS:	117 (1903-2020)
RECORD:	10,378 – 7,840 .570 W-L %
PLAYOFF APPEARANCES:	55
PENNANTS:	40
WORLD CHAMPIONSHIPS:	27
WINNINGEST MANAGER:	Joe McCarthy 1,460 – 867 .636 W-L %

© 2020 They Played Baseball for the Yankees?

And their 16,215 home runs not only lead all other teams, but are nearly 2,000 more than the next team on the list.

Everyone knows of the greats who have had long careers with the Yankees: Hall of Famers like Babe Ruth, Lou Gehrig, Yogi Berra, Mickey Mantle and White Ford; as well as contemporaries like Derek Jeter and Mariano Rivera, to name just a few.

But did you know that at one time or another, 15 other Hall of Famers have made stops at Yankee stadium? Including two from the NFL? Not to mention players who went on to become four of the greatest managers in Major League Baseball history, and two sets of brothers? So I hope you'll enjoy discovering the interesting stories surrounding how and why these, and over 35 other players you may have forgotten about or maybe even didn't know, spent time in a Yankees uniform, and what they did while they were wearing it.

You'll find player stories broken up alphabetically into three categories based on their time with the Yankees:

- *"The Start of Something Big"*: players who began their career as a Yankee but excelled elsewhere.

- *"Hello and Goodbye"*: players who had short tenures as a Yankee during their career.

- *"The End of the Line"*: players who flourished with other teams but retired as a Yankee.

The Start of Something Big

After observing the 10 players that make up this category, players who started their careers as a Yankee, you'll notice one other thing that several have in common: they excelled once they left.

So although these players were all rookies with the Yankees, they weren't around long enough, or didn't do much when they were there, for many people to remember.

- Hal Chase
- Bobby Cox
- Dazzy Vance
- Deion Sanders
- George Halas
- J.T. Snow
- Jackie Jenson
- Lefty O'Doul
- Leo Durocher
- Lew Burdette

Hal Chase

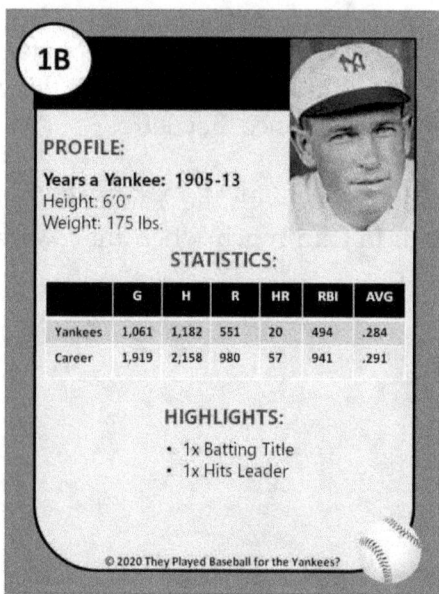

PROFILE:
Years a Yankee: 1905-13
Height: 6'0"
Weight: 175 lbs.

STATISTICS:

	G	H	R	HR	RBI	AVG
Yankees	1,061	1,182	551	20	494	.284
Career	1,919	2,158	980	57	941	.291

HIGHLIGHTS:
- 1x Batting Title
- 1x Hits Leader

© 2020 They Played Baseball for the Yankees?

During his 15 year career, "Prince Hal" played for five teams, beginning with the New York Highlanders in 1905.

Known particularly for his fielding abilities, many consider Chase as the first true star of the New York franchise that eventually became the Yankees. Babe Ruth, Cy Young and Walter Johnson all named Chase the best first baseman they ever saw.

Despite these accolades, Chase's legacy was tainted by repeated allegations of alleged corruption, including gambling on baseball games and engaging in suspicious play in order to deliberately throw games he played in. None of these allegations were ever substantiated, however.

Regardless, it took eight and a half seasons before Chase wore out his welcome in New York, but during that time he established himself as one of the biggest stars in baseball. Although the Highlanders went through six managers, including Chase himself (1910-11), and only posted two winning seasons, "Prince Hal" finished among the American League top ten leaders four times in RBIs, three times in batting average, and twice in stolen bases. Despite that, Chase was sent to the Chicago White Sox for light hitting infielders Babe Borton and Rollie Zeider on June 1, 1913. In 1916 with the Cincinnati Reds, Chase won the National League batting title with a .339 average.

In his 8+ years in New York, Chased batted .284 in 1,062 games while hitting 20 home runs and driving in 494.

They Played Baseball for the Yankees?

Bobby Cox

There's no doubt that Bobby Cox will best be remembered in Major League Baseball history as a manager and not a ball player. Leading the Atlanta Braves to the 1995 World Series championship as well as five National League Pennants, Cox took home four Manager-of-the-Year awards on his way to the Major League Baseball Hall-of-Fame in 2014.

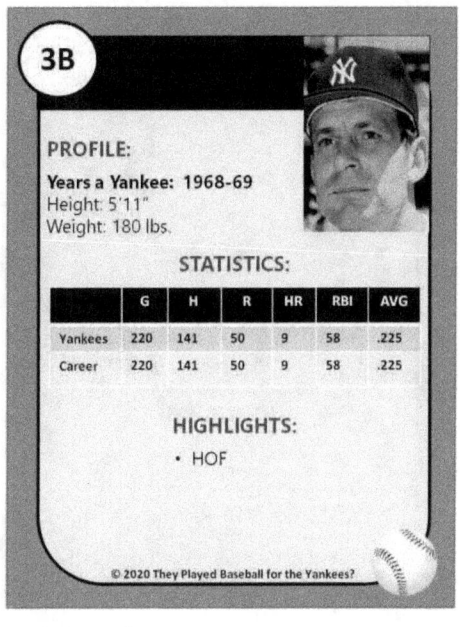

PROFILE:
Years a Yankee: 1968-69
Height: 5'11"
Weight: 180 lbs.

STATISTICS:

	G	H	R	HR	RBI	AVG
Yankees	220	141	50	9	58	.225
Career	220	141	50	9	58	.225

HIGHLIGHTS:
- HOF

© 2020 They Played Baseball for the Yankees?

As a player, however, Cox' career began and ended with the Yankees after two injury-filled seasons. Originally signed with the Los Angeles Dodgers, Cox was acquired by the Atlanta Braves after he was unable to make the Dodgers' major league team. After failing to play a game with the Braves as well, Atlanta traded Cox to the Yankees on December 7, 1967.

Cox played two seasons for the Yankees, mostly at third base, and hit .225 over 200 games. Because of bad knees, Cox platooned with several players during the 1968 and 1969 seasons before being released by the Yankees on September 22, 1970. He was re-signed by the Yankees on July 17, 1971 but was released again for good on August 28, 1971. He never played in a game during that time.

They Played Baseball for the Yankees?

Dazzy Vance

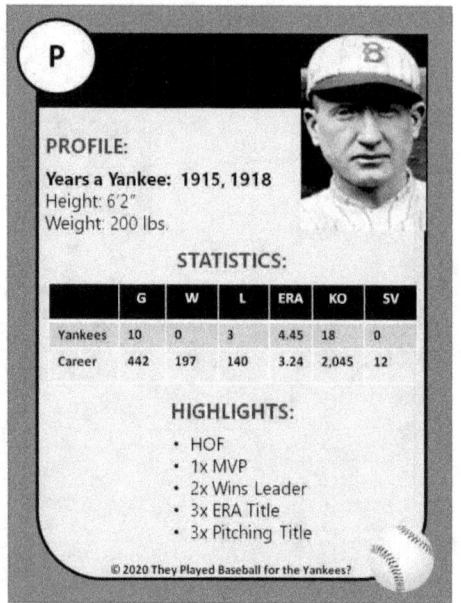

Twenty-four year old Charles Arthur "Dazzy" Vance made his major league debut in 1915 with a whimper, pitching in one game with the Pittsburgh Pirates and three games with the Yankees before an arm injury resurfaced after he had pitched four games in six days the year before in the minors. After taking two years off to recover, Vance returned to the Yankees in 1918, only to be released after pitching poorly in two games.

His career seemingly over, Vance was playing poker in 1920 when he banged his arm on the edge of the table, causing intense pain. A visit to a doctor revealed bone chips in his previously injured elbow that were undetected years earlier. After having them removed, a now healthy Vance resumed his Hall of Fame-to-be baseball career at age 31, pitching the bulk of the next 13 years with the Brooklyn Dodgers.

Upon retiring after the 1935 season, Vance had led the National League in earned run average three times, wins twice, and established a record by leading the league in strikeouts in seven consecutive years (1922–1928). He retired with a 197–140 record, 2,045 strikeouts and a 3.24 earned run average, all after pitching in only 33 innings of big league ball before age 30.

Vance's best individual season came in 1924, when he led the National League in wins (28), strikeouts (262) and earned run average (2.16) en route to winning the National League MVP award. He set a then-National League record for strikeouts in a nine-inning game when he fanned 15 Chicago Cubs on August 23, 1924. A year later he struck-out 17 batters in a 10-inning game.

Deion Sanders

"Neon" Deion was originally drafted by the Kansas City Royals in the sixth round of the 1985 draft, but he never signed with them. Instead, the New York Yankees selected Sanders in the 30th round of the 1988 Major League Baseball draft, and he signed with the team on June 22. After spending a few months in minor league ball, Sanders made his major league debut on May 31, 1989.

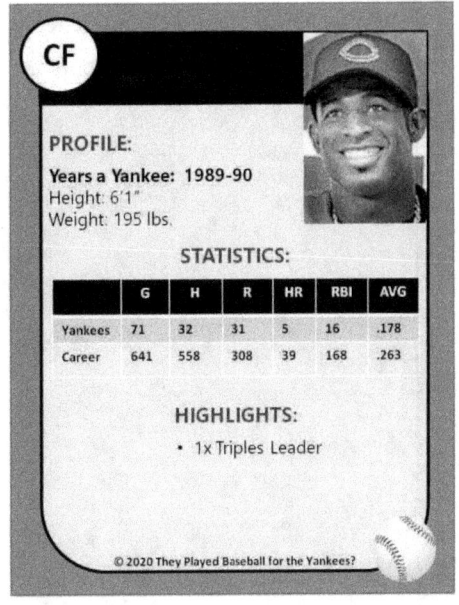

PROFILE:
Years a Yankee: 1989-90
Height: 6'1"
Weight: 195 lbs.

STATISTICS:

	G	H	R	HR	RBI	AVG
Yankees	71	32	31	5	16	.178
Career	641	558	308	39	168	.263

HIGHLIGHTS:
- 1x Triples Leader

© 2020 They Played Baseball for the Yankees?

In April 1989, Sanders was drafted by the Atlanta Falcons of the NFL, and he would begin a dual career playing in both professional leagues until 2001 when he quit baseball. During one week in the 1989 season, Sanders hit a major league home run and scored a touchdown in the NFL becoming the only player ever to do so. Sanders is also the only man to play in both a Super Bowl and a World Series.

Sanders made the Yankee's Opening Day roster for the 1990 season, but by mid-July was unsure if he would remain with the Yankees or report to training camp for the upcoming NFL season. After the Yankees balked at Sander's $1 million salary request for the 1991 season, negotiations ended and Sanders left the team to join the Falcons, finishing the 1990 season with a .158 batting average and three home runs in 57 games. In September 1990, the Yankees placed Sanders on waivers with the intention of giving him his release. Sanders subsequently signed with the Atlanta Braves in 1991, which allowed him to play for both of the city's professional teams.

George Halas

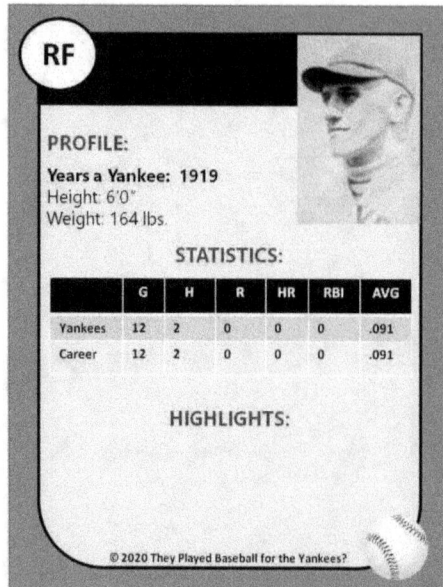

"Papa Bear" Halas was a highly rated prospect going into his 1919 rookie season with the New York Yankees, so much so that a Chicago sportswriter wrote *"There is a young man on the New York roster that is being overlooked and will make New York sit up and take notice next summer. That young man is George Halas."*

But Halas's major-league debut was delayed when he injured a hip during a spring-training game. Hampered by his injury, he had just two hits in 22 at-bats once the 1919 season began. In July, with permission from the Yankees, Halas traveled to Youngstown, Ohio, to visit a sports-injury specialist who was able to immediately fix Halas's hip problem. But when Halas rejoined the Yankees later that year, it was too late. *"A fellow named Babe Ruth was playing in my place,"* Halas would later explain.

That may have been a blessing in disguise, as on September 17, 1920, Halas was part of a group representing 11 different professional football teams that congregated in an automotive showroom in Canton, Ohio, to discuss the formation of the very first professional football league. When the meeting concluded, the American Professional Football Association (APFA) had been formed. Two years later, the name would be changed to the National Football League (NFL).

Halas would be one of the original head coaches in the NFL, leading the Chicago Bears from 1923 until 1967 when he retired at the age of 72. During his tenure, Halas' teams won 324 games and eight NFL Championships.

J.T. Snow

On June 5, 1989, Jack Thomas Snow was drafted by the New York Yankees out of the University of Arizona in the 5th round of the 1989 amateur draft, and signed with them six days later. While at Arizona, Snow was teammates with future professional major leaguers Kenny Lofton, Scott Erickson and Trevor Hoffman.

Snow broke into the Majors with the Yankees at the end of the 1992 season where he played in seven games, knocking out two hits in 14 at-bats while driving in one run.

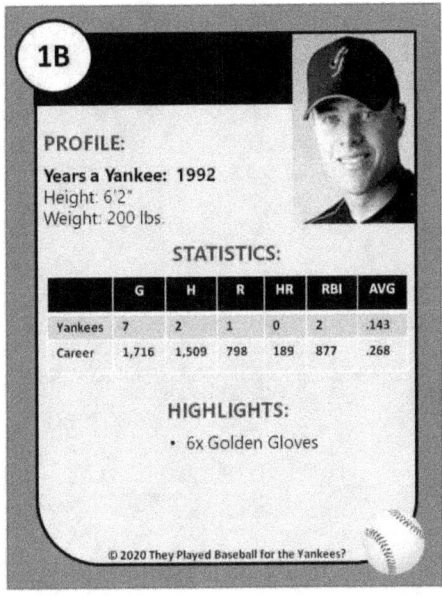

1B

PROFILE:
Years a Yankee: 1992
Height: 6'2"
Weight: 200 lbs.

STATISTICS:

	G	H	R	HR	RBI	AVG
Yankees	7	2	1	0	2	.143
Career	1,716	1,509	798	189	877	.268

HIGHLIGHTS:
- 6x Golden Gloves

© 2020 They Played Baseball for the Yankees?

On December 6, 1992, the Yankees traded Snow along with Jerry Nielsen and Russ Springer to the California Angels for pitcher Jim Abbott.

Incidentally, if you are a professional football fan, the name "Jack Snow" may have caught your eye. That's because J.T. was not the first person in his family to play professional sports. His father Jack Snow senior played ten years in the NFL as an All-Pro wide receiver for the Los Angeles Rams.

They Played Baseball for the Yankees?

Jackie Jensen

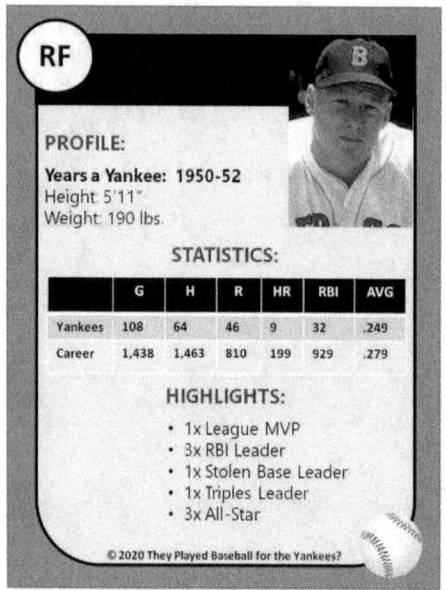

PROFILE:
Years a Yankee: 1950-52
Height: 5'11"
Weight: 190 lbs.

STATISTICS:

	G	H	R	HR	RBI	AVG
Yankees	108	64	46	9	32	.249
Career	1,438	1,463	810	199	929	.279

HIGHLIGHTS:
- 1x League MVP
- 3x RBI Leader
- 1x Stolen Base Leader
- 1x Triples Leader
- 3x All-Star

© 2020 They Played Baseball for the Yankees?

In 1949, Jensen left college after his junior year and signed with the Oakland Oaks in the Pacific Coast League. His contract – along with Billy Martin's – was sold to the New York Yankees in 1950 with the intention of Jensen backing up Joe DiMaggio in centerfield. Jensen would only play in 108 games for the Yankees over the next three seasons, and appeared as a pinch runner for Bobby Brown in the eighth inning of Game 3 of the 1950 World Series against the Philadelphia Phillies. He did not appear in the 1951 Series against the New York Giants.

A productive spring, and the retirement of DiMaggio, put Jensen in center field to start the 1952 season for the Yankees, with a rookie named Mickey Mantle in right field. However, after a 2-for-19 start, Jensen was abruptly traded to the Washington Senators in a six-player deal on May 3. Yankees manager Casey Stengel would later call the trade the worst the Yankees made during his tenure with the club.

Bucky Harris, Washington's manager, put Jensen in right field and batted him third the rest of the season. Jensen responded with a breakout season, hitting .286 with 10 home runs and 80 runs batted in. Hitting .314 at the All-Star break, Stengel chose Jensen as a reserve outfielder for the American League All-Stars.

After being traded to the Boston Red Sox in 1954, Jensen went on to win a league MVP and three RBI titles before retiring in 1960. Jensen hit .249 with the Yankees in 108 games.

They Played Baseball for the Yankees?

Lefty O'Doul

In 1918, Francis "Left" O'Doul pitched in 49 games with the AAA San Francisco Seals, posting a 12-8 record and a 2.63 earned run average. Liking what they saw, the New York Yankees drafted O'Doul on September 21, 1918.

O'Doul appeared in 19 games with the Yankees in 1919, pitching only three times, but remained with the club all season pinch-hitting, tossing batting practice and doing whatever was needed.

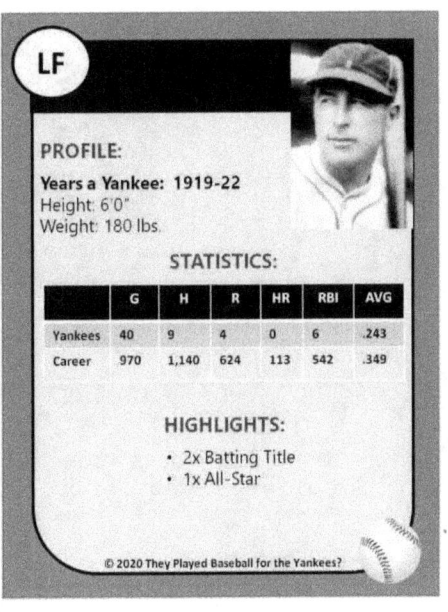

LF

PROFILE:
Years a Yankee: 1919-22
Height: 6'0"
Weight: 180 lbs.

STATISTICS:

	G	H	R	HR	RBI	AVG
Yankees	40	9	4	0	6	.243
Career	970	1,140	624	113	542	.349

HIGHLIGHTS:
- 2x Batting Title
- 1x All-Star

© 2020 They Played Baseball for the Yankees?

Just a few days before Babe Ruth was purchased by the Yankees in 1919, he and O'Doul met in an exhibition game in California. O'Doul struck Ruth out in his first two at bats, but Ruth homered the next time up. O'Doul appeared in only 13 games for the Yankees in 1920, but again stayed on the roster all season. On June 23, 1922 the Yankees traded three players, $50,000 and a player-to-be-named to the Red Sox for Joe Dugan and Elmer Smith. O'Doul would be notified on September 29 that he was the player-to-be-named later. In 1924, O'Doul was converted into an outfielder, which is where his career really flourished.

As an outfielder, O'Doul won two batting titles and nearly hit .400 in 1929 when he batted .398 after playing in all 154 games. He finished with a .349 career batting average, fourth-best in history. After leaving the majors, he returned to the west coast and managed for more than 20 years, amassing more than 2,000 wins, a total surpassed by only eight men in minor league history. He was recognized as one of the game's great hitting instructors.

Leo Durocher

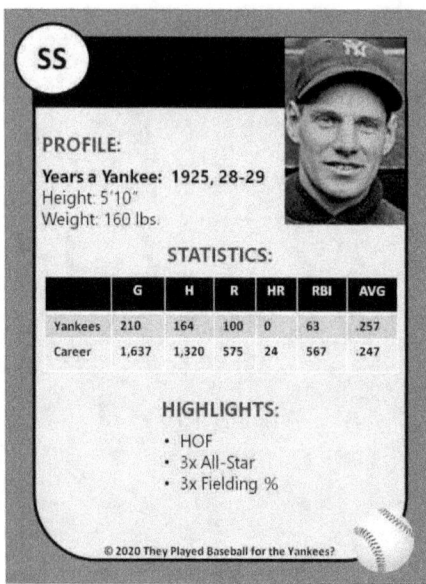

PROFILE:
Years a Yankee: 1925, 28-29
Height: 5'10"
Weight: 160 lbs.

STATISTICS:

	G	H	R	HR	RBI	AVG
Yankees	210	164	100	0	63	.257
Career	1,637	1,320	575	24	567	.247

HIGHLIGHTS:
- HOF
- 3x All-Star
- 3x Fielding %

© 2020 They Played Baseball for the Yankees?

After being scouted by the New York Yankees, Leo "the Lip" Durocher broke into professional baseball with the minor league Hartford Senators of the Eastern League in 1925. He was called up to the Yankees and played in two games that year. Durocher spent two more seasons in the minors, playing for the Atlanta Crackers of the Southern Association in 1926 and St. Paul Saints of the American Association in 1927 before rejoining the Yankees in 1928.

As a starter in 1928, he was nicknamed "The All-American Out" by Babe Ruth. Durocher helped the team win their second consecutive World Series title in 1928, but then, after demanding a raise, was sold to the Cincinnati Reds on February 5, 1930. Durocher spent the remainder of his professional career in the National League where he became a three-time All-Star and fielding percentage leader for shortstops.

Beginning in 1939, Durocher became a player/manager for the Brooklyn Dodgers until 1945 when he retired from playing. "The Lip" went on to manage until 1973 before retiring with the Chicago Cubs at the age of 67. During his managerial career, Durocher led his teams to three pennants and one World Series title, while amassing 2,008 wins.

During his playing career with the Yankees, Durocher hit .257 over three seasons, while collecting 164 hits and driving in 63 runs.

Lew Burdette

Born in Nitro, West Virginia, Burdette was signed by the New York Yankees in 1947. After making two relief appearances for the team in September 1950, the 23 year-old was traded to the Braves in August 1951 for 33 year-old, four-time 20-game winner Johnny Sain.

Burdette's career blossomed with Milwaukee, winning 179 games for the Braves, including 20 wins in 1958 and a league-leading 21 wins in 1959. Burdette also won 19 games twice, pitched a no-hitter, and took home an earned run average title while being named to three All-Star teams.

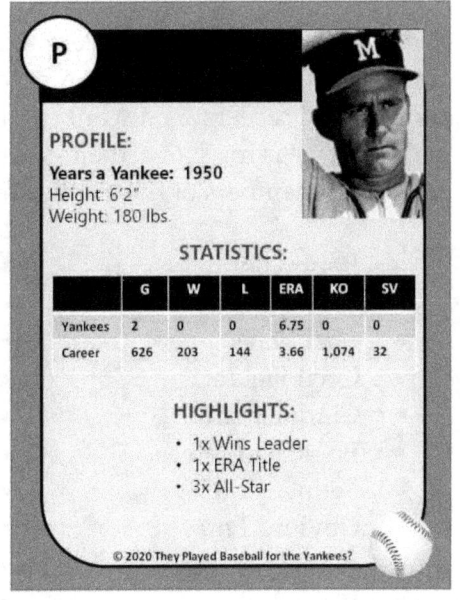

PROFILE:
Years a Yankee: 1950
Height: 6'2"
Weight: 180 lbs.

STATISTICS:

	G	W	L	ERA	KO	SV
Yankees	2	0	0	6.75	0	0
Career	626	203	144	3.66	1,074	32

HIGHLIGHTS:
- 1x Wins Leader
- 1x ERA Title
- 3x All-Star

© 2020 They Played Baseball for the Yankees?

Burdette was the winning pitcher on May 26, 1959 when the Pittsburgh Pirates' Harvey Haddix pitched a perfect game against the Braves for 12 innings, only to lose in the 13th. Burdette threw a 1–0 13-inning shutout, scattering 12 hits to get the win. In the ensuing offseason, Burdette joked, "*I'm the greatest pitcher that ever lived. The greatest game that was ever pitched in baseball wasn't good enough to beat me, so I've got to be the greatest!*"

In an 18-year career, Burdette posted a 203–144 record with 1,074 strikeouts and a 3.66 earned run average while compiling 158 complete games and 33 shutouts.

Sain would pitch five seasons for the Yankees, winning 33 games and losing 20, while posting a 3.67 earned run average.

Hello and Goodbye

These well-known players were technically Yankees, but were only around for a handshake and a quick cup of coffee. None began or ended their careers as a Yankee, and some were around for only part of a season. Nevertheless, these 25 big name players will always be members of the Yankee family.

- Bobby Bonds
- Branch Ricky
- Carl Mays
- Cecil Fielder
- Clark Griffith
- Enos Slaughter
- Felipe Alou
- Gaylord Perry
- Ivan Rodriquez
- Jack Clark
- Joe Niekro
- John Candelaria
- Johnny Sain
- Jose Canseco
- Ken Griffey Sr.
- Lee Smith
- Luis Tiant
- Matty Alou
- Pete Incaviglia
- Phil Niekro
- Randy Johnson
- Sal Maglie
- Sam McDowell
- Tim Raines
- Toby Harrah

They Played Baseball for the Yankees?

Bobby Bonds

After breaking in with the San Francisco Giants in 1968, Bobby Bonds would soon find himself being groomed to replace the legendary, but aging, Willie Mays. Talk about pressure! Bonds responded by hitting over 20 home runs in six of his seven seasons as a Giant. In addition, he was an All-Star twice and a three-time Golden Glove winner.

Bonds also had the distinction of leading the league in strikeouts three times, striking out over 130 times in each of his seasons in San Francisco.

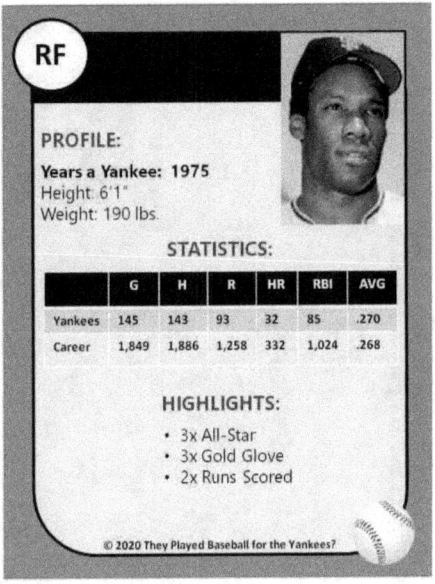

PROFILE:
Years a Yankee: 1975
Height: 6'1"
Weight: 190 lbs.

STATISTICS:

	G	H	R	HR	RBI	AVG
Yankees	145	143	93	32	85	.270
Career	1,849	1,886	1,258	332	1,024	.268

HIGHLIGHTS:
- 3x All-Star
- 3x Gold Glove
- 2x Runs Scored

© 2020 They Played Baseball for the Yankees?

Bobby Mercer, a rookie with the New York Yankees also had big shoes to fill. Mickey Mantle, the Hall-of-Fame legend had retired in 1969, and Mercer was being counted on to replace him as well. Unfair as that was, Mercer responded by hitting 22 or more home runs his first five seasons as a Yankee. He drove in over 90 runs three times, and hit over .300 twice. He was also an All-Star four of his first six seasons.

After the 1974 season, however, the Yankees were looking for more right-handed power, and the Giants more consistency. So the two clubs surprised the baseball world by swapping their star outfielders in a straight up trade of $100,000 superstars.

Bonds only played one year in New York, hitting .270 with 32 home runs and 85 RBIs while making the All-Star team before unexpectedly being shipped to the California Angels for Mickey Rivers and Ed Figueroa after the 1975 season.

They Played Baseball for the Yankees?

Branch Rickey

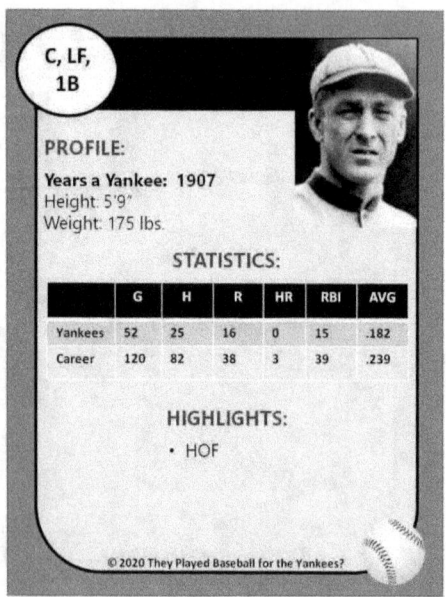

Similar to Bobby Cox, Leo Durocher, and Clark Griffith, three other subjects in this book, Branch Rickey made his real mark in baseball off the field rather than on it.

Rickey made his major league debut in 1905 with the St. Louis Browns before being sold to the New York Highlanders in 1907. Unable to hit consistently with the New York club, Rickey finished the 1907 season with a meager .182 batting average. His defense wasn't much better, as one opposing team stole 13 bases in one game while Rickey was behind the plate, which was an American League record at the time. Rickey injured his throwing arm during the season and retired as a player at the end of the year.

Rickey went on to manage the St. Louis Browns and Cardinals from 1913-1925, sporting a 597-664 record with both teams before being bumped up to the Cardinals front office where he found his true role in baseball.

In 1942, Rickey became President and General Manager of the Brooklyn Dodgers, where he performed his most memorable, and historical, act of his career. On August 28, 1945, he signed Jackie Robinson to break baseball's color barrier, which had been an unwritten rule since the 1880s.

They Played Baseball for the Yankees?

Carl Mays

During a 15-year career with the Boston Red Sox, New York Yankees, Cincinnati Reds, and New York Giants, Carl Mays compiled a 207-126 record with 29 shutouts, 862 strikeouts. In addition, he had a 2.92 earned run average at a time when the league earned run average was 3.48. He won twenty or more games five times, including a league high 27 in 1921.

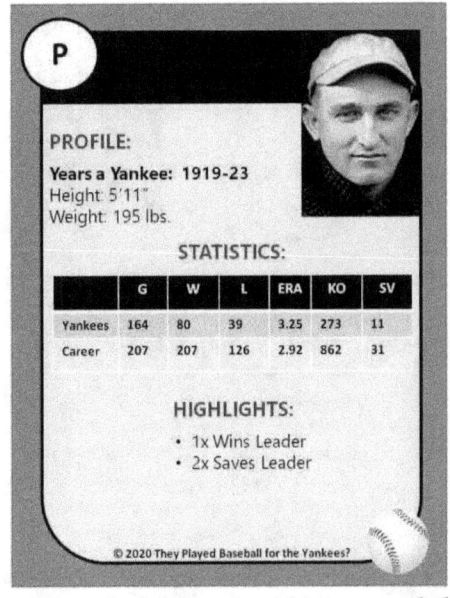

PROFILE:
Years a Yankee: 1919-23
Height: 5'11"
Weight: 195 lbs.

STATISTICS:

	G	W	L	ERA	KO	SV
Yankees	164	80	39	3.25	273	11
Career	207	207	126	2.92	862	31

HIGHLIGHTS:
- 1x Wins Leader
- 2x Saves Leader

© 2020 They Played Baseball for the Yankees?

Mays was also pretty good with a bat, hitting five home runs and driving in 110 runs while supporting a lifetime .268 batting average, unheard of for a pitcher these days. Mays once tossed two nine-inning complete game victories on the same day (August 30, 1918) for the Red Sox, beating the Philadelphia Athletics 12-0 and 4-1. Something else non-existent in today's baseball world.

Unfortunately, Mays' primarily memory as a Yankee may be for throwing the pitch that killed Ray Chapman of the Cleveland Indians on August 16, 1920. Chapman became the only major league player to die as a direct result of an on-field injury. By that time, Mays, one of the first submarine style pitchers in baseball history, already had a reputation of brushing batters off the plate, even getting into an altercation with Ty Cobb in 1915. After a few close pitches, Cobb threw his bat towards Mays and the two began exchanging unpleasantries. When order was restored and Cobb stepped back into the batter's box, Mays proceeded to hit him on the wrist with a pitch.

Mays pitched in 164 games for the Yankees, winning 80 of them while supporting a 3.25 earned run average.

They Played Baseball for the Yankees?

Cecil Fielder

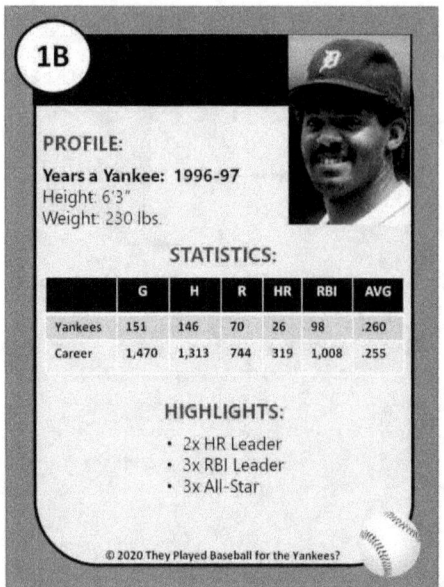

After beginning his career with four part-time seasons as a Toronto Blue Jay, Cecil "Big Daddy" Fielder enjoyed his greatest success during his sub-sequent six-year tenure with the Detroit Tigers.

As a Tiger, Fielder had four consecutive 30-homer and 100-RBI seasons. During the strike-shortened 1994 season, he had 28 home runs and 90 RBIs in 109 games. He also became the first Tiger to hit at least 25 home runs in six consecutive seasons. Fielder was also a member of the 1990, 1991, and 1993 All-Star teams.

On July 31, 1996, Fielder was traded to the New York Yankees for Rubén Sierra and Matt Drews. Fielder's acquisition was integral to the Yankees' World Series championship that year, as he won the Babe Ruth Award for most outstanding performance in the 1996 postseason. Fielder stayed with the Yankees in 1997 where he hit 13 home runs and drove in 61 runs, before signing as a free agent with the Anaheim Angels and Cleveland Indians in 1998.

In 1999. Fielder finished his career back where it started when he signed with the Blue Jays. Toronto would cut Fielder in spring training, however, and Fielder soon retired.

During his short tenure as a Yankee, Fielder played in 151 games, blasting 26 home runs, driving in 98 while hitting .260.

They Played Baseball for the Yankees?

Clark Griffith

Few individuals in the history of baseball can boast of a career to rival that of Clark Griffith's. In terms of duration, it was one of the longest ever for a player, manager and executive, spanning nearly 70 years. Griffith is the only man in major league history to serve as player, manager, and owner for at least 20 years in each role.

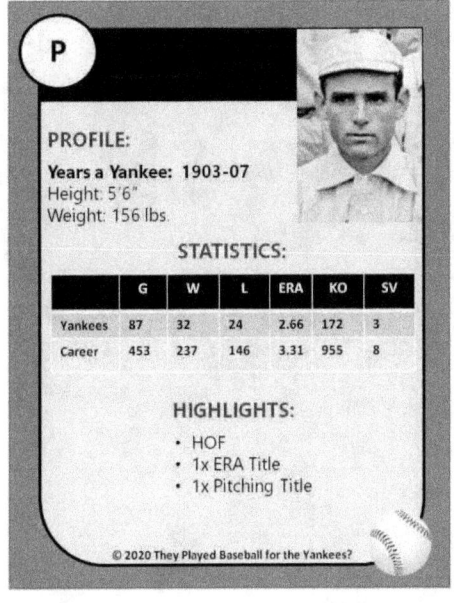

Nicknamed "The Old Fox", Griffith began his major league playing career with the St. Louis Browns (1891). He joined the New York Highlanders in 1903, and after four years in the Big Apple, ended his career in Cincinnati in 1909.

Following his playing days, Griffith became the primary owner of the Washington Senators from 1920 until his death in 1955. He led the Senators to a World Series championship in 1924 and a return trip in 1925, only to lose to the Pittsburgh Pirates after the Senators squandered a 3-1 series lead.

Although primarily known for his time as the owner of the Senators, Griffith was an above average pitcher during his 15 year professional career, winning over 20 games in seven of the eight seasons between 1894 and 1901, while snagging the earned run average title in 1898 with a 1.88 mark.

During his tenure with New York, Griffith pitched in 87 games, winning 32 of them. He supported an impressive 2.66 earned run average as well, all while between the ages of 35 and 37.

Enos Slaughter

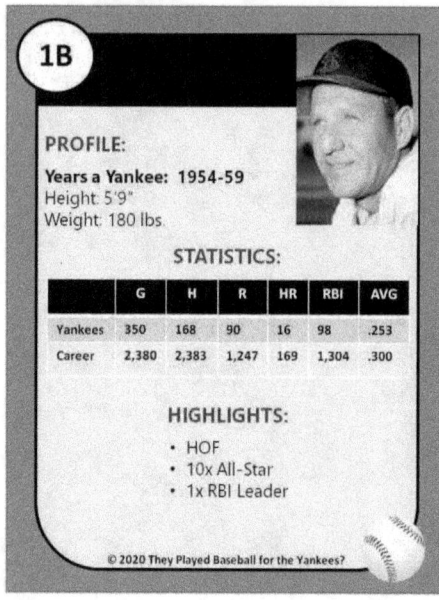

PROFILE:
Years a Yankee: 1954-59
Height: 5'9"
Weight: 180 lbs.

STATISTICS:

	G	H	R	HR	RBI	AVG
Yankees	350	168	90	16	98	.253
Career	2,380	2,383	1,247	169	1,304	.300

HIGHLIGHTS:
- HOF
- 10x All-Star
- 1x RBI Leader

© 2020 They Played Baseball for the Yankees?

Enos "Country" Slaughter came up with the St. Louis Cardinals in 1938, and for the next 15 years was a fixture on the Red Birds team. Following 10 consecutive All-Star appear-ances, the 37 year-old was traded to the Yankees two days before the 1954 season.

"Country" would miss over a month of the season after crashing into the outfield wall at Yankee Stadium, fracturing his left wrist in three places. After being limited to only 22 games in right field and sporadically used as a pinch hitter, the Yankees traded Slaughter to the Kansas City Athletics prior to the 1956 season. New York, however, reacquired Slaughter on August 25 of that year for the waiver price. To make room for Slaughter on the roster, the Yankees released the popular Phil Rizzuto the same day.

Slaughter played sparingly for the Yankees over the next four seasons, but still left his mark. His three-run homer off Roger Craig in game three of the 1956 World Series powered the Yankees to a 5-3 victory. In game five, Slaughter was in right field during teammate Don Larson's historic perfect game.

The Yankees released the 43 year-old Slaughter near the end of the 1959 campaign, where he finished the season in Milwaukee before retiring.

They Played Baseball for the Yankees?

Felipe Alou

On June 8, 1958, Felipe Alou became the second Dominican player in major league history, playing right field and leading off for the San Francisco Giants. He singled and doubled off Cincinnati's Brooks Lawrence in his first two at-bats. Three days later, hit his first home run off Pittsburgh's Vernon Law.

In September 1963, Alou's younger brother Jesús was recalled from Triple-A Tacoma to join Felipe and their other brother Matty in San Francisco. Late in a game on September 15, Jesús and Matty replaced Willie Mays and Willie McCovey in the field, joining Felipe to create an all-Alou outfield. The brothers repeated this two more times that month. This three brother outfield feat has never been repeated in Major League Baseball since.

In 1966, Matty and Felipe finished one-two in the National League Batting Title, with Matty hitting .342 and Felipe .327.

In 1970, the 35 year-old Felipe was the elder statesman on a young Oakland A's team filled with up and coming stars. Just a few days into the 1971 season, Oakland dealt Alou to the Yankees for two young pitchers. Alou played most of the next three years in New York alternating between outfield and first base, playing in 344 games while hitting .289, .278 and .236 respectively. The Yankees waived Alou on September 6, 1973.

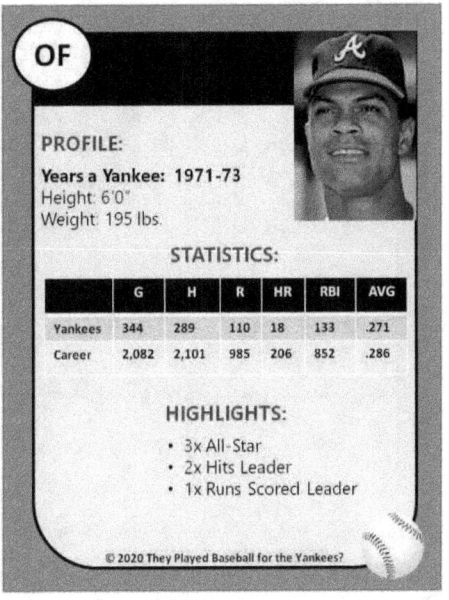

OF

PROFILE:
Years a Yankee: 1971-73
Height: 6'0"
Weight: 195 lbs.

STATISTICS:

	G	H	R	HR	RBI	AVG
Yankees	344	289	110	18	133	.271
Career	2,082	2,101	985	206	852	.286

HIGHLIGHTS:
- 3x All-Star
- 2x Hits Leader
- 1x Runs Scored Leader

© 2020 They Played Baseball for the Yankees?

Gaylord Perry

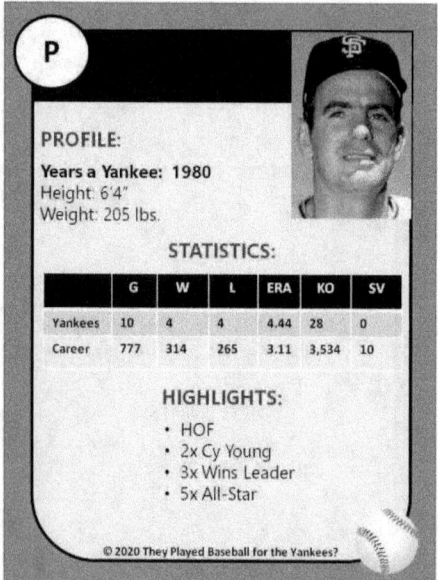

During his 22-year baseball career, Gaylord Perry compiled 314 wins, 3,534 strikeouts, and a 3.11 Earned Run Average. In 1991, he was elected to the Baseball Hall of Fame in his third year of eligibility.

Perry, a five-time All-Star, was the first pitcher to win the Cy Young Award in both leagues, winning it in the American League with the Cleveland Indians in 1972 and in the National League with the San Diego Padres in 1978. While pitching for the Seattle Mariners in 1982, Perry became the 15th member of the 300 win club.

Despite all of these impressive accomplishments, Perry is probably best known for his allegedly throwing of a spit ball (doctoring a baseball with a foreign substance). Despite the accusations, Perry was never ejected for the illegal practice until August 23, 1982, in his 21st season in the majors. But it is more than likely the reason why it took him three years to make the Hall of Fame.

On August 24, 1980, Perry was dealt to the Yankees for pitcher Ken Clay, putting Perry in his first pennant race since 1971. He finished the season 4-4 for the division-winning Yankees, but did not pitch in the team's three-game playoff loss to the Royals. Almost two months after trading for him, the Yankees granted the 42 year-old Perry his free agency on October 23rd.

Ivan Rodriquez

In 1991, Ivan "Pudge" Rodriguez was 19 years-old when he made his major league debut for the Texas Rangers. "Pudge" would go on to catch 88 games in 1991, the second most ever by a teenaged catcher.

Some 20 years later, Rodriguez would retire after the 2011 season, but not before capturing several major league records for a catcher.

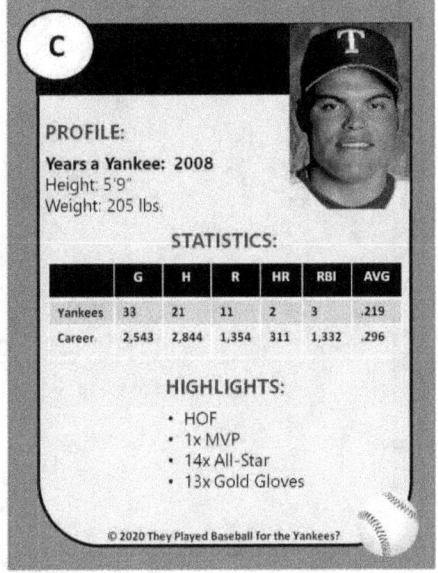

On June 17, 2009, Rodriguez caught his 2,227th game, passing Carlton Fisk. In 1996 he hit 44 doubles breaking Mickey Cochrane's mark 66 years earlier. The same year he had 639 at-bats to break the single season total by Johnny Bench.

In 1999, "Pudge" set a new American League record for home runs in a single season among catchers with 35, and was the first catcher to have more than 30 home runs, 100 runs batted in, and 100 runs scored in a single major league season.

On July 30, 2008, the Yankees, needing to replace an injured Jorge Posada, traded reliever Kyle Farnsworth to the Detroit Tigers for 36 year-old Rodríguez. Sharing catching duties with Jose Molina, Rodríguez would only start 26 of the remaining 55 games. Also, for the first time in his career, Rodriguez had to choose a different jersey number as his customary number 7 had been retired by the Yankees for Mickey Mantle. He finished the year with a .278 batting average, but only .219 while wearing the number 12 as a Yankee. "Pudge" was granted his free agency after the end of the season.

Jack Clark

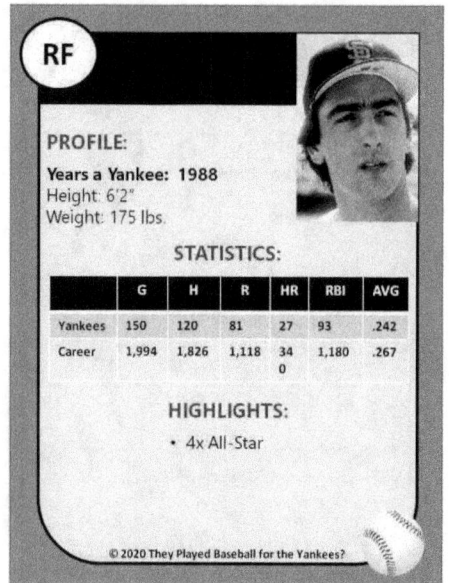

From 1975 through 1992, "Jack the Ripper" Clark played for the San Francisco Giants (1975–84), St. Louis Cardinals (1985–87), New York Yankees (1988), San Diego Padres (1989–90) and Boston Red Sox (1991–92).

During his prime, Clark was one of the most feared right-handed hitters in the National League, winning the Silver Slugger Award in 1985 and 1987. A four-time All-Star in an 18-season career, Clark was a .267 hitter with 340 home runs and 1,180 RBI in 1,994 games. He also collected 1,118 runs, 332 doubles, 77 stolen bases, 1,262 bases on balls and 1,826 hits in 6,847 at-bats.

Prior to the 1988 season, Clark signed a two-year contract with the Yankees after three successful years in St. Louis, including a 1987 season where he hit 35 home runs with 106 RBIs. Because of the presence of Don Mattingly at first base, Clark was primarily used as a designated hitter.

Although Clark enjoyed playing for manager Billy Martin, he didn't get along with Martin's successor, Lou Piniella. So at the end of the 1988 season he requested a trade. On October 24, Clark was sent with Pat Clements to the San Diego Padres for Stan Jefferson, Jimmy Jones and Lance McCullers.

Clark hit .242 with 27 home runs and 93 RBIs during his one season with the Yankees.

Joe Niekro

When Joe Niekro took the field on April 25, 1969 with the expansion San Diego Padres, he had the distinction of being the first player in Padre history to wear number 37. On June 27, he became the first Padre hurler ever to pitch a complete game shutout.

Along with his older brother Phil, the Niekros won 539 major league games (221 for Joe), the highest total for a brother combination in baseball history.

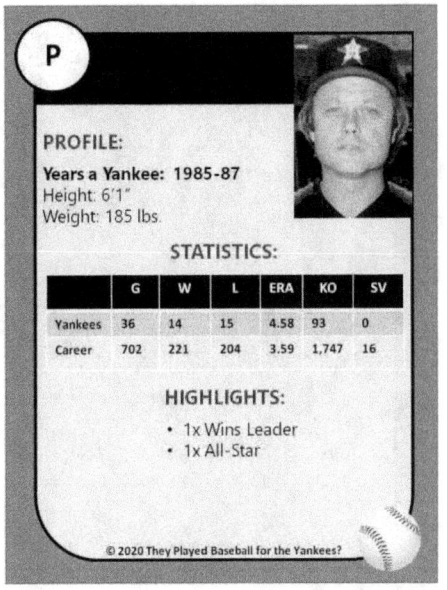

PROFILE:
Years a Yankee: 1985-87
Height: 6'1"
Weight: 185 lbs.

STATISTICS:

	G	W	L	ERA	KO	SV
Yankees	36	14	15	4.58	93	0
Career	702	221	204	3.59	1,747	16

HIGHLIGHTS:
- 1x Wins Leader
- 1x All-Star

© 2020 They Played Baseball for the Yankees?

In 1973, Niekro began the first of two seasons with brother Phil in Atlanta before the Houston Astros purchased his contract from the Braves in 1975. It was with the Astros that Niekro perfected his knuckleball and blossomed into a dominant pitcher in the National League. In 1979 and 1980, Niekro posted 21–11 and 20–12 records to become the first Astros pitcher ever to win 20 games in consecutive seasons. The year 1979 also saw the Niekro brothers tie for the most wins in Major League Baseball with 21, marking the only year that two brothers shared the honor.

In 1985, after going 9–12 with a 3.72 earned run average for the Astros, the 40 year-old Niekro was traded to the Yankees for Jim Deshaies and two players to be named later. In his three seasons with New York, where he was briefly reunited with brother Phil, Niekro went 14–15 with a 4.58 earned run average in 188.2 total innings. He was traded to the Minnesota Twins on June 7, 1987 for catcher Mark Salas.

In a bit of irony, the only home run Niekro hit in his 22-year major league career was against his brother Phil on May 29, 1976.

John Candelaria

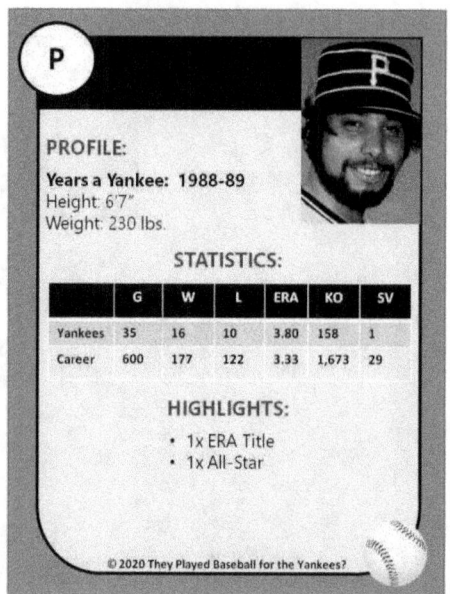

On June 8, 1975, 21 year-old New York native John Candelaria made his major-league debut against the San Francisco Giants. Even though he lost 3-1, he pitched well enough to stay in the Pittsburgh Pirate rotation, and on June 20 at Shea Stadium, pitched in hometown New York for the very first time. Candelaria would earn his first major-league win by throwing his first complete game to beat the New York Mets, 5-1.

On August 9, 1976, Candelaria no-hit the Los Angeles Dodgers 2-0 for the first no-hitter pitched by a Pirate in Pittsburgh since Nick Maddox in 1907. Candelaria had his best season in 1977, when he was 20-5 with a 2.34 earned run average as a member of the 1979 World Series champion Pirates team.

In 1988, after being guaranteed a spot in their starting rotation, the 34 year-old Candelaria signed as a free agent with the Yankees. After starting well with a 13-7 record, Candelaria came down with knee pain in August 1988, and after surgery for cartilage damage was done for the year. Although he started 1989 in the Yankee rotation, Candelaria returned to the disabled list in May after more knee surgery and missed another three months. He returned to the Yankee bullpen for a short time before being traded in late August 1989 to the Montreal Expos for third baseman Mike Blowers.

In 1993, 39 year-old Candelaria would finish his career back where it started in Pittsburgh.

Johnny Sain

As a member of the Milwaukee Braves, Johnny Sain was argu-ably the top pitcher in the National League from 1946 to 1948 with a 65-41 record and 2.77 earned run average. After notching win totals of 20, 21 and 24 in three consecutive seasons, a first in franchise history, Sain experimented with a screwball in 1949 and subsequently injured his arm.

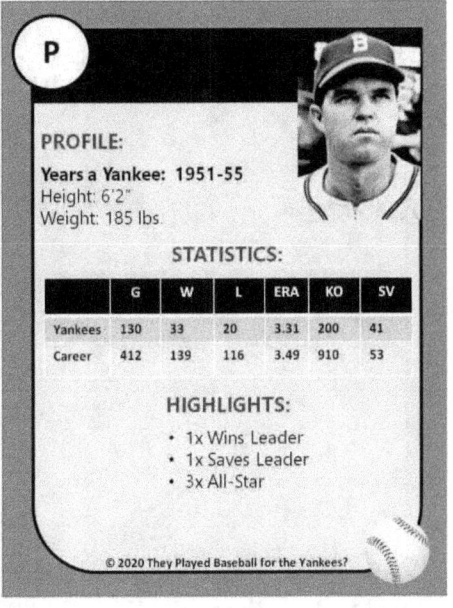

After a 10-17 1949 season, Sain bounced back with a 20-13 record in 1950. His earned run average continued to climb, however, and after a 5-13 start in 1951, the 33 year-old Sain was dealt to the Yankees for prospect Lew Burdette. With his arm still not 100%, the Yankees compensated by making Sain a spot starter and reliever, so only about half of his appearances were starts — 16 of 35 in 1952 and 19 of 40 in 1953. He completed half of his starts, eight in 1952 and ten in 1953, and relieved the rest of the time. In 1954, his last full year in pinstripes, all 45 of his appearances were in relief, and he saved a league-leading 22 games to become just the second pitcher to win 20 games in one season and save 20 in another. Only four other pitchers have done that since.

On May 11, 1955, Sain was traded with Enos Slaughter to the Kansas City Athletics for Sonny Dixon. Two months later, Sain was released by the A's and soon after retired at the age of 37.

The Yankees hired Sain in 1961 as pitching coach, a role he would hold for 17 years with several teams. During his time as a coach, he would help sixteen pitchers win 20-games.

They Played Baseball for the Yankees?

Jose Canseco

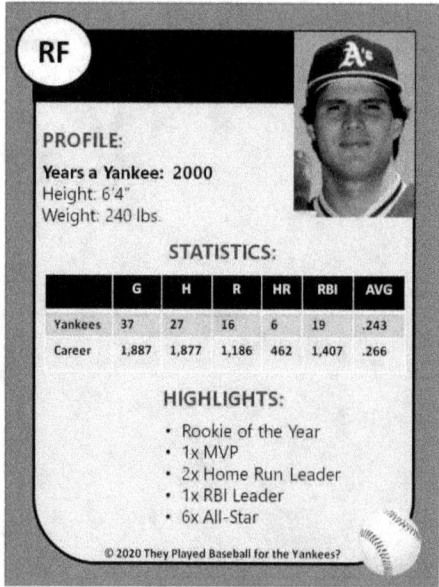

During his time with the Oakland A's, Jose Canseco Capas Jr. established himself as one of the premier power hitters in the game. He won the Rookie of the Year (1986), Most Valuable Player award (1988), and was a six-time All-Star.

In 1988, Canseco became the first player to hit 40 home runs and steal 40 bases in one season. At one time, Canseco was the all-time leader in home runs among Latino players, and was the first player to hit 30 home runs for four different teams.

Canseco began the 2000 season with the Tampa Bay Devil Rays. But after hitting only nine home runs in 61 games, he was released and claimed off waivers by the Yankees that August. Later, it was revealed that Yankees General Manager Brian Cashman made the claim to prevent the A's, Boston Red Sox and Toronto Blue Jays, who were in a close race with the Yankees, from acquiring Canseco.

In a lesser role with the Yankees, the 35 year-old Canseco split duties as an outfielder, designated hitter and pinch hitter. Canseco played in 37 games for New York, hitting .243 with six home runs. He struck out in his only plate appearance in the 2000 World Series against the New York Mets, but earned his second World Series ring when the Yankees defeated the Mets in five games. His first was with the A's in 1989.

The Yankees granted Canseco his free agency following the 2000 season.

They Played Baseball for the Yankees?

Ken Griffey, Sr.

Ken Griffey made his major league debut on August 25, 1973 with the Cincinnati Reds, and had his best season three years later when his .336 average finished second in the National League behind Bill Madlock of the Chicago Cubs.

After helping the Reds win consecutive World Series titles in 1975 and 1976, Griffey averaged .304 in his next four seasons before the Reds sent him to the Yankees in late 1981 for two prospects. Griffey played in 562 games over the next five injury-plagued seasons for the pinstripes, hitting .285 overall as a utility first baseman and outfielder. In 1983, Griffey hit .306 with 11 homers and 46 RBIs, his best as a Yankee. Three years later, in June 1986, the 36 year-old Griffey was traded with Andre Robertson to the Atlanta Braves in exchange for Claudell Washington and Paul Zuvella. Griffey rejoined the Reds for a brief time in 1988.

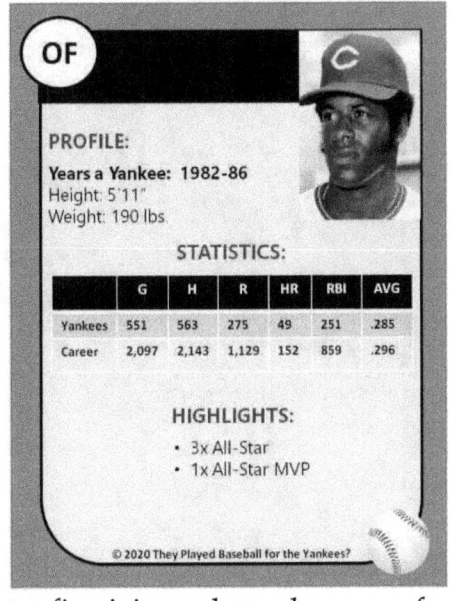

OF

PROFILE:
Years a Yankee: 1982-86
Height: 5'11"
Weight: 190 lbs.

STATISTICS:

	G	H	R	HR	RBI	AVG
Yankees	551	563	275	49	251	.285
Career	2,097	2,143	1,129	152	859	.296

HIGHLIGHTS:
- 3x All-Star
- 1x All-Star MVP

© 2020 They Played Baseball for the Yankees?

Despite these accomplishments, Griffey is probably best known as being the father of Hall-of-Famer Ken Griffey Jr. In late August 1990, Griffey Sr. was released by the Reds and was quickly signed by the Seattle Mariners, the same team his son played for. On August 31, the two made history against the Kansas City Royals, as they became the first father-and-son duo to play in a major league game together. The 40 year-old Griffey Sr. and 20 year-old Griffey Jr. hit back-to-back singles during their first at-bats in the bottom of the first. On September 14 at Anaheim they did one better, hitting back-to-back home runs off of Kirk McCaskill of the Angels.

Lee Smith

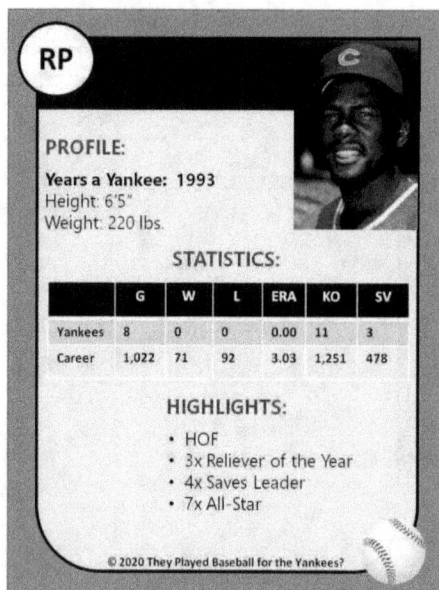

PROFILE:
Years a Yankee: 1993
Height: 6'5"
Weight: 220 lbs.

STATISTICS:

	G	W	L	ERA	KO	SV
Yankees	8	0	0	0.00	11	3
Career	1,022	71	92	3.03	1,251	478

HIGHLIGHTS:
- HOF
- 3x Reliever of the Year
- 4x Saves Leader
- 7x All-Star

© 2020 They Played Baseball for the Yankees?

In 1993, the Yankees were just 1½ games behind the Toronto Blue Jays for the division lead when they acquired 35 year-old All-Star reliever/closer Lee Smith for Rich Batchelor on August 31, 1993. Smith was nearly perfectly for the last month of the season with the Yankees, as he did not allow a single run and picked up three saves and 11 strikeouts in the eight games he pitched in. As a team, however, the Yankees faltered the remainder of the season, and Toronto pulled away to win the division. Smith filed for free agency after the season and signed with the Baltimore Orioles in 1994.

Prior to his tenure with the Yankees, Smith was one of the best relievers in baseball. Nine times he saved over 30 games in a season (11 total in his career), and twice over 40. In his 18 major-league seasons, the right-hander played with eight different teams. He won saves titles in both leagues, three times in the National League with the Chicago Cubs and St. Louis Cardinals, and once in the American League with Baltimore. In 1991, when he set a National League record with 47 saves for the St. Louis Cardinals, he was runner-up for the league's Cy Young Award.

When he retired after the 1997 season, he was the major leagues' career save leader with 478. Smith was voted into the Baseball Hall of Fame on December 9, 2018.

Luis Tiant

On the final day of the 1978 season, the Boston Red Sox needed a win and a Yankee loss to force a one game playoff. Catfish Hunter and the Yankees lost in Cleveland while Boston's Luis Tiant dazzled the Fenway crowd with a two-hitter against the Blue Jays. The Yankees would win the playoff game, but Tiant showed his worth in helping his team get there by going 13-8 during the season.

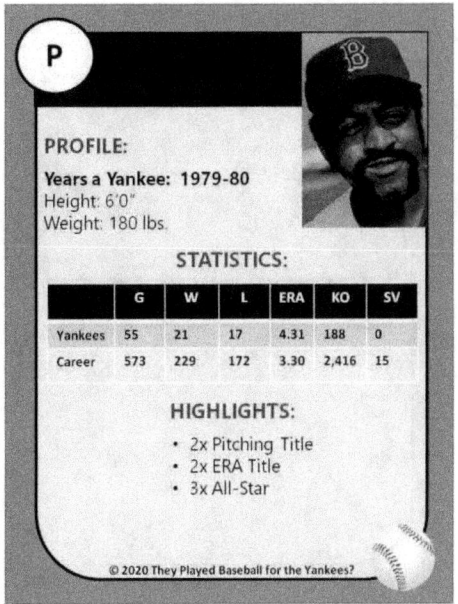

PROFILE:
Years a Yankee: 1979-80
Height: 6'0"
Weight: 180 lbs.

STATISTICS:

	G	W	L	ERA	KO	SV
Yankees	55	21	17	4.31	188	0
Career	573	229	172	3.30	2,416	15

HIGHLIGHTS:
- 2x Pitching Title
- 2x ERA Title
- 3x All-Star

© 2020 They Played Baseball for the Yankees?

In the offseason, the Red Sox would only offer the 38 year-old free agent a one-year contract. After the rival Yankees presented him with a two year contract plus a 10-year scouting deal, Tiant accepted the offer. The move was not popular with some of the Red Sox players, as one would state, "*They tore out our heart and soul.*"

In 1979 with the Yankees, Tiant won 13 games while posting a 3.91 earned run average, including a 3-2 victory over the Red Sox in September. His record fell to 8-9 in 1980, and the Yankees let him go after the season. He signed with the Pittsburgh Pirates in 1981 before retiring after the 1982 season with the California Angels.

Prior to his time with the Yankees, Tiant won 20 games three times for the Red Sox and once for the Cleveland Indians. He won earned run average titles in 1968 with the Indians (1.60) and 1972 with the Red Sox (1.91). With the Indians, Tiant had the rare distinction of winning 20 games in 1968 (21-9) while losing 20 the following year (9-20) for a Cleveland team that lost 99 games.

They Played Baseball for the Yankees?

Matty Alou

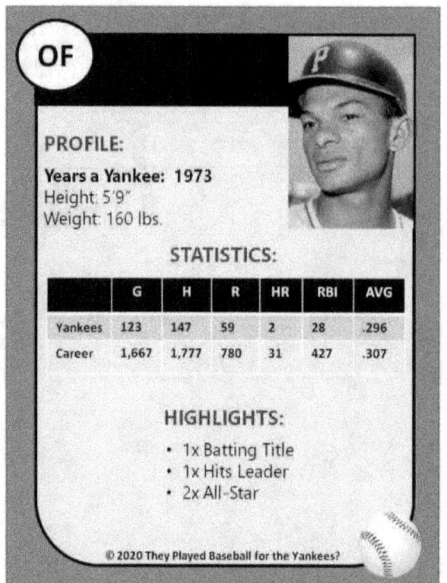

Mateo "Matty" Alou was the middle of a trio of baseball-playing brothers that included the older Felipe and younger Jesús. They were the first set of brothers to play together in the same outfield and all bat in the same half-inning in major league history, both with the San Francisco Giants in 1963.

Alou was traded by the Giants to the Pittsburgh Pirates before the 1966 season, where he received instruction from expert hitting instructor Harry Walker The training helped Alou become a formidable hitter and an integral member of the Pirates team.

Subsequently, Alou won the 1966 National League batting title, and finished in the top five four more times after that. His best year was 1969, when he led the major leagues in at-bats (698), doubles (41), and hits (231). As of 2020, his 231 hits remain the highest total by any National League player since Joe Medwick's 237 in 1937.

In 1972, after winning a World Series title with the Oakland Athletics, the A's traded the 34 year-old Alou to the Yankees where he briefly reunited with brother Felipe. After the team fell out of contention in 1973, Alou was sold by the Yankees to the St. Louis Cardinals on September 6. During his time in New York, Alou hit .296 in 123 games as the starting right fielder. He finished his career with the San Diego Padres, retiring after the 1974 season with an impressive .307 career average over 15 seasons.

Pete Incaviglia

In his first five seasons with the Texas Rangers, Pete Incaviglia hit at least 20 home runs each year. After brief stops in Detroit and Houston in 1991 and 1992, where his playing time and production dropped, his career received a much needed boost when he was signed by the Philadelphia Phillies before the 1993 season.

In just 368 at-bats, Incaviglia hit 24 home runs and drove in a career-best 89 runs for the Phillies, who reached the World Series that year, only to lose to the Toronto Blue Jays.

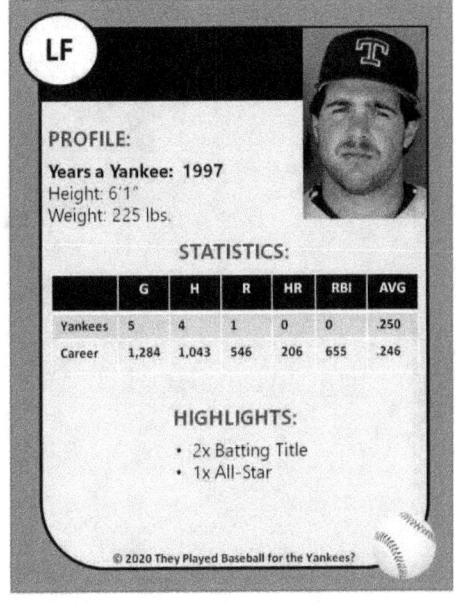

LF

PROFILE:
Years a Yankee: 1997
Height: 6'1"
Weight: 225 lbs.

STATISTICS:

	G	H	R	HR	RBI	AVG
Yankees	5	4	1	0	0	.250
Career	1,284	1,043	546	206	655	.246

HIGHLIGHTS:
- 2x Batting Title
- 1x All-Star

© 2020 They Played Baseball for the Yankees?

Eleven days after being released by the Baltimore Orioles in 1997, the Yankees signed the 33 year-old Incaviglia to a minor-league contract. He was assigned to AAA Columbus, which was his first time in the minors.

After three games with Columbus, Incaviglia was called up to a Yankees squad ravaged with injuries. He started well with New York, collecting three hits in his first game, an 8-3 win over the Minnesota Twins. After collecting just one hit in his next 12 at bats, and with Tim Raines coming off the disabled list, Incaviglia was designated for assignment on Aug. 12. He was released by the Yankees three days later.

Incaviglia played for both Detroit and Houston a second time in his final major league season in 1998.

They Played Baseball for the Yankees?

Phil Niekro

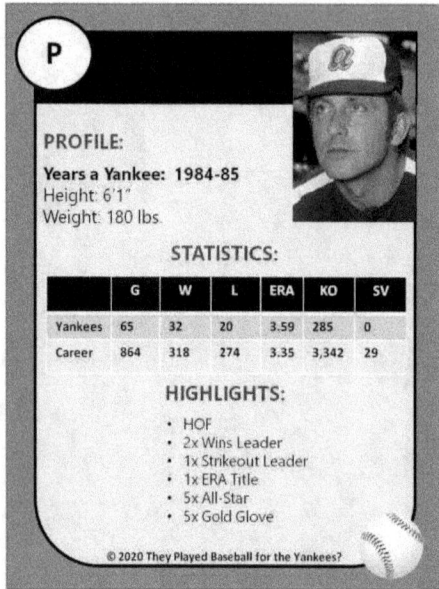

Phil "Knucksie" Niekro played 24 seasons in Major League Baseball, 20 of them with the Milwaukee/Atlanta Braves. His longevity is attributed to his knuckleball, a difficult pitch to master but easy on the arm.

Niekro's 318 career victories are the most by a knuckleball pitcher and rank 16th on the all-time wins list. He won the National League Gold Glove Award five times, led the league in victories twice, and earned run average once.

Phil and his younger brother Joe Niekro amassed 539 wins between them, the most combined wins by brothers in baseball history.

Niekro was the last major league pitcher to have both won and lost 20 or more games in the same season, which he did in 1979 when he finished with 21 wins and 20 losses. That season, Phil and brother Joe were National League co-leaders in wins.

After the Braves released him in 1983, Niekro signed with the Yankees in 1984. In his first of two seasons in the Bronx, "Knucksie" won 16 games and made his fifth and final All-Star appearance.

The next season, Niekro gained entry into the 300 win club with a shutout over the Toronto Blue Jays on October 6, 1985. He finished the season with a 16-12 record, the final time he won 15 or more games in a single season. The 46 year-old Niekro was released by the Yankees before the start of the 1986 season.

Randy Johnson

At 6'10", the aptly nicknamed "Big Unit", won 303 games in his 22-year career. His 4,875 strikeouts place him second all-time behind Nolan Ryan and are the most by a left-hander. And on May 18, 2004, at the age of forty, Johnson became the oldest pitcher in Major League Baseball history to throw a perfect game. He is also one of eighteen pitchers in history to record a win against all 30 franchises.

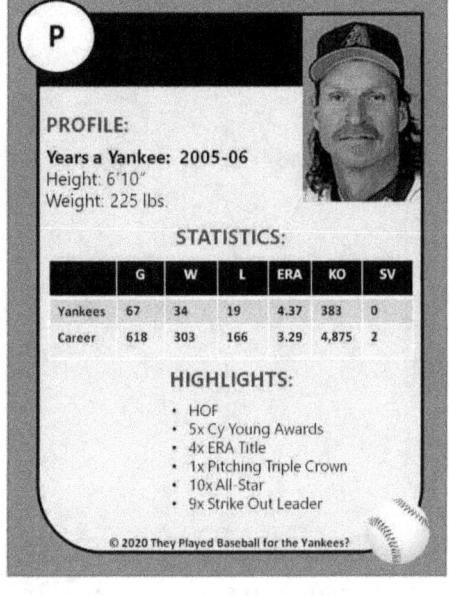

In January 2005, the Arizona Diamondbacks traded the 41 year-old Johnson to the Yankees for Javier Vázquez, Brad Halsey, Dioner Navarro, and cash. Johnson pitched Opening Day for the Yankees on April 3, 2005. Although inconsistent during the early part of the season, Johnson regained his dominance in late 2005, finishing the season at 17–8 with a 3.79 earned run average, and was second in the American League with 211 strikeouts.

Johnson began 2006 well, but again struggled with consistency, allowing five or more runs in seven of his first 18 starts of the season. After a better second half, Johnson finished the season with a 17–11 record, but a high 5.00 earned run average.

In January 2007, almost two years to the day that Arizona had traded him to New York, the Yankees traded Johnson back to the Diamondbacks for Luis Vizcaino, Ross Ohlendorf, Alberto Gonzalez and Steven Jackson,. This was, in part, according to the New York Times, to allow Johnson to be closer to his family after the death of his brother.

Sal Maglie

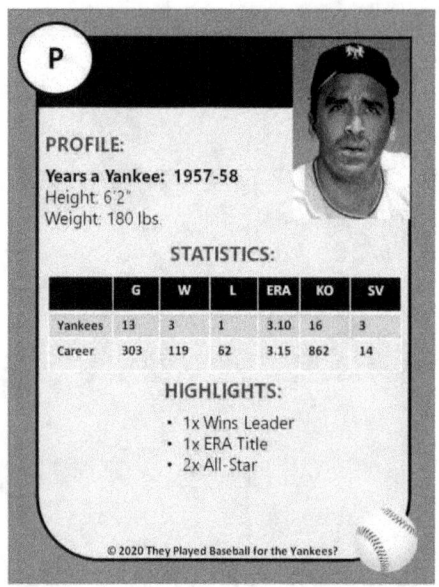

PROFILE:
Years a Yankee: 1957-58
Height: 6'2"
Weight: 180 lbs.

STATISTICS:

	G	W	L	ERA	KO	SV
Yankees	13	3	1	3.10	16	3
Career	303	119	62	3.15	862	14

HIGHLIGHTS:
- 1x Wins Leader
- 1x ERA Title
- 2x All-Star

© 2020 They Played Baseball for the Yankees?

In 1956, the Cleveland Indians sold 39 year-old Sal Maglie to the Brooklyn Dodgers for $100 in what would be regarded as one of the greatest bargains in baseball history. Later that year, Maglie tossed a no-hitter on the road to helping Brooklyn capture the National League crown. In what would be the last highlight of his career, and one frequently forgotten, Maglie pitched eight innings and allowed the Yankees only two runs on five hits during Don Larsen's perfect game five of the 1956 World Series.

Towards the end of the 1957 season, Maglie was waived by the Dodgers after posting a 6-6 record. A few weeks later, the Dodgers moved to Los Angeles. In the meantime, the Yankees claimed the 40 year-old Maglie, making him the last player to wear the uniform of all three New York teams. Maglie went 1-0 with a 1.93 earned run average, pitching well during the final month of the season. Nonetheless, the Yankees passed him on to the St. Louis Cardinals in 1958, where Maglie stumbled to a 3-7 record in his final major league season. When spring training ended in 1959, the Cards gave Maglie his unconditional release.

Maglie opened a new chapter in his baseball life in 1961 when he became pitching coach for the Boston Red Sox. In 1962, Boston pitchers Bill Monbouquette and Earl Wilson both tossed no-hitters, giving credit to Maglie for their improved pitching performances.

Sam McDowell

"Sudden Sam" McDowell was an imposing 6'5" lefty nicknamed such because of his slow wind up and electrifying fastball that dominated the American League in the late 1960's. From 1965 through 1971, McDowell was an all-star six times, won an earned run average title, and was a 20-game winner in 1970 for a Cleveland Indians team that won only 76 games.

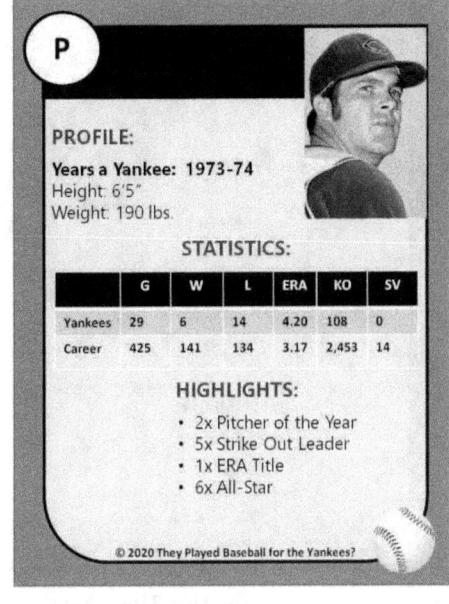

PROFILE:
Years a Yankee: 1973-74
Height: 6'5"
Weight: 190 lbs.

STATISTICS:

	G	W	L	ERA	KO	SV
Yankees	29	6	14	4.20	108	0
Career	425	141	134	3.17	2,453	14

HIGHLIGHTS:
- 2x Pitcher of the Year
- 5x Strike Out Leader
- 1x ERA Title
- 6x All-Star

© 2020 They Played Baseball for the Yankees?

By the time 1972 rolled along, however, the 29 year-old McDowell's fastball began to lose steam, and his dominance started to fade. After a sub-par 1971 season, and following some contract issues with the Indians, McDowell demanded a trade. He was subsequently dealt to the San Francisco Giants for Gaylord Perry.

After two lackluster seasons with the Giants, where he was primarily used in relief, McDowell was sold to the New York Yankees in 1973 and was moved back into the starting rotation. He started the season hot, winning five of his first six starts, but failed to win another game after that. He finished the season with a 5-8 record. Things got even worse for McDowell in 1974. After a stint on the disable list because of a slipped disc, he posted a 1-6 record with a 4.69 earned run average before the Yankees released him at the end of the season.

McDowell pitched three months for the Pittsburgh Pirates in 1975 before retiring from baseball at the age of 32.

Tim Raines

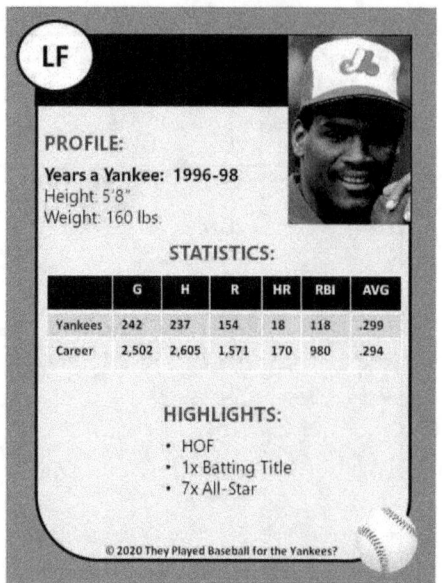

PROFILE:
Years a Yankee: 1996-98
Height: 5'8"
Weight: 160 lbs.

STATISTICS:

	G	H	R	HR	RBI	AVG
Yankees	242	237	154	18	118	.299
Career	2,502	2,605	1,571	170	980	.294

HIGHLIGHTS:
- HOF
- 1x Batting Title
- 7x All-Star

© 2020 They Played Baseball for the Yankees?

In a 23-year Hall-of-Fame career, Tim Raines played in 2,502 games accumulating 2,605 hits in 8,872 at bats for a .294 career batting average. One of the predominant lead-off men in the 1980's, Raines stole at least 70 bases in each of his first six full seasons with the Montreal Expos (1981–1986). He lead the National League in stolen bases from 1981 to 1984, with a career high of 90 steals in 1983. Raines batted over .300 in five full seasons and over .320 in his next two, winning the 1986 National League batting title with a .334 average.

With 808 steals in his career, Raines has the fourth-highest total in major league history behind Rickey Henderson, Lou Brock and Ty Cobb.

On December 28, 1995, after acquiring him from the Expos five years earlier, the Chicago White Sox traded the 36 year-old Raines to the Yankees for minor league pitcher Blaise Kozeniewski. In a bit of good timing for Raines, the Yankees had just started their late-1990s championship run when he joined their roster.

Injuries would plague Raines his three years with the team (1996-98), limiting him to an average of 81 games per season. Despite this, he played in his first World Series in 1996, and won World Series rings in 1996 and 1998. His cumulative batting average for the three seasons in New York was .299.

Toby Harrah

After a 1982 season, in which he hit 25 home runs and batted .304 enroute to making his fourth American League All-Star team, Toby Harrah had high hopes for his final contract year with the Cleveland Indians.

However, two off-field incidents in February of 1983 would affect Harrah's season. On February 19th, a fire damaged his home, forcing his family into a hotel for four months. The day after the fire, Harrah signed autographs at a baseball card show in Dallas. When he returned to his hotel room, he received word that his father had been killed in a car accident earlier that day. Harrah would also miss a month of the season when he broke his hand for the second time, courtesy of an errant pitch.

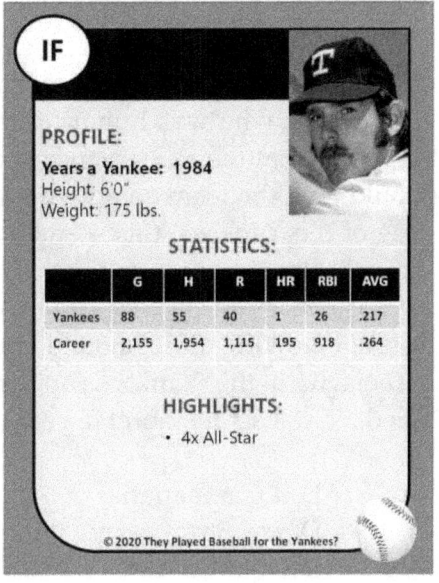

IF

PROFILE:
Years a Yankee: 1984
Height: 6'0"
Weight: 175 lbs.

STATISTICS:

	G	H	R	HR	RBI	AVG
Yankees	88	55	40	1	26	.217
Career	2,155	1,954	1,115	195	918	.264

HIGHLIGHTS:
• 4x All-Star

© 2020 They Played Baseball for the Yankees?

Harrah's time in Cleveland came to an end when he agreed to waive his no-trade clause and was dealt to the Yankees on February 5, 1984 for George Frazier, Otis Nixon and Rick Browne. Harrah became a part-time player in New York, sharing time with Roy Smalley at third base. After batting only .217 in 88 games in 1984, the Yankees traded Harrah back to the Texas Rangers, the franchise he started with in 1971, for Billy Sample and Eric Dersin.

When he retired from the Rangers after the 1986 season, Harrah was the last active major leaguer to have played for the Washington Senators franchise. He was also the last player to bat for the Senators in their final game on September 30, 1971. The Senators would move to Arlington, Texas and become the Texas Rangers in 1972.

The End of the Line

Throughout baseball history, it would not be unusual for a team fighting for a playoff spot to bring on a player in the twilight of their career who was hungry for one final championship run. The hope was that their experience and motivation to win one final time would give the team an added edge during a pennant drive. In the case of the Yankees, this seemed to happen a lot in the 1990's and early 2000's. And more often than not, the move worked!

So the following are 10 notable players who, although ending their careers with the Yankees, enjoyed their most productive, glory-filled, or at least memorable years with other teams.

- Bert Campaneris
- Darryl Strawberry
- Dwight Gooden
- Frank Chance
- Home Run Baker
- Jeff Reardon
- John Mayberry
- Johnny Mize
- Kevin Brown
- Paul Waner

They Played Baseball for the Yankees?

Bert Campaneris

On July 23, 1964, Bert "Campy" Campaneris made his major league debut and hit a home run in his first at-bat off the first pitch ever thrown to him. Six innings later, Campaneris rip-ped another home run, making him one of only five players in major league history to hit two home runs in his first game.

On September 8, 1965, Campaneris became the first player to play every position in a major league game, including pitcher. On the mound, he pitched ambidextrously, throwing lefty to left-handed hitters, and righty to right-handed hitters.

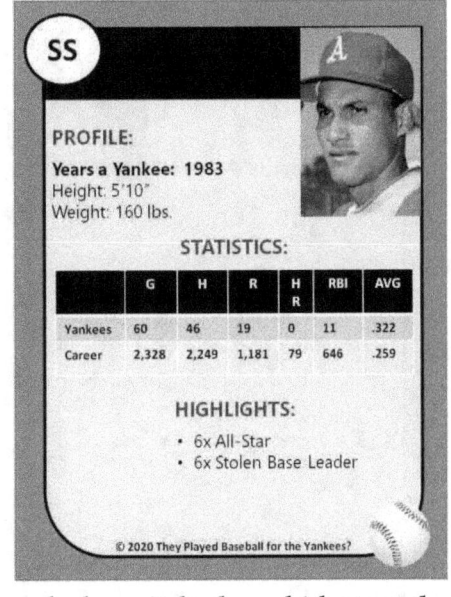

SS

PROFILE:
Years a Yankee: 1983
Height: 5'10"
Weight: 160 lbs.

STATISTICS:

	G	H	R	HR	RBI	AVG
Yankees	60	46	19	0	11	.322
Career	2,328	2,249	1,181	79	646	.259

HIGHLIGHTS:
- 6x All-Star
- 6x Stolen Base Leader

© 2020 They Played Baseball for the Yankees?

During the next 18 years, Campaneris won three World Series titles, and six stolen base titles. He appeared in six All-Star games, mostly for the Kansas City/Oakland A's.

After stints with the Texas Rangers and California Angels from 1977 to 1981, Campaneris spent the 1982 season in the Mexican League, before returning to the majors for a last hurrah in 1983 with Billy Martin's Yankees. He batted a career-high .322 in 60 games at second and third base for New York before retiring at the age of 41 in November, 1983.

They Played Baseball for the Yankees?

Darryl Strawberry

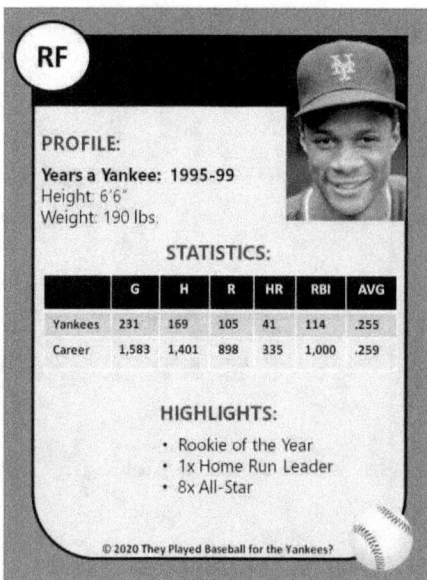

PROFILE:
Years a Yankee: 1995-99
Height: 6'6"
Weight: 190 lbs.

STATISTICS:

	G	H	R	HR	RBI	AVG
Yankees	231	169	105	41	114	.255
Career	1,583	1,401	898	335	1,000	.259

HIGHLIGHTS:
- Rookie of the Year
- 1x Home Run Leader
- 8x All-Star

© 2020 They Played Baseball for the Yankees?

After winning National League Rookie-of-the-Year in 1983 with the New York Mets, Darryl Strawberry went on to blast 26 or more home runs in each of the next eight seasons. He belted a league high 39 home runs in 1988, making him one of the most feared hitters in baseball.

A lucrative offer by the Los Angeles Dodgers drew the free agent to the west coast after the 1990 season. By 1992, at the age of 29, Strawberry had belted 280 home runs and was earning comparisons to Hank Aaron. Injuries and personal problems affected Strawberry's production, however, and he wound up only playing in 75 games the next two seasons before being released by the Dodgers in May of 1994.

After finishing the 1994 season with the San Francisco Giants, Strawberry signed with the Yankees in 1995. Showing flashes of his former self, Strawberry belted 11 home runs in a part-time role to help New York win the World Series in 1996 alongside former Mets teammates Dwight Gooden and David Cone.

In 1998, Strawberry hit 24 home runs and again helped the Yankees win the World Series, playing 100 games for the first time since 1991. After being diagnosed with colon cancer at the end of 1998, Strawberry attempted a comeback in 1999 following cancer treatment that resulted in his playing in only 24 regular season games. In the post season however, Strawberry contributed several key hits during the American League Division Series that helped the Yankees win another World Series. Strawberry would retire after the season at the age of 37.

Dwight Gooden

As a 19 year-old rookie with the New York Mets in 1984, Dwight "Doc" Gooden posted a 17-9 record and 2.60 earned run average on his way to winning the 1984 National League Rookie of the Year award. Gooden managed to top that the next season by leading all National League pitchers with a 24-4 record, 1.53 earned run average, and 268 strikeouts. This rare pitcher's "triple crown" feat earned Gooden the 1985 Cy Young award.

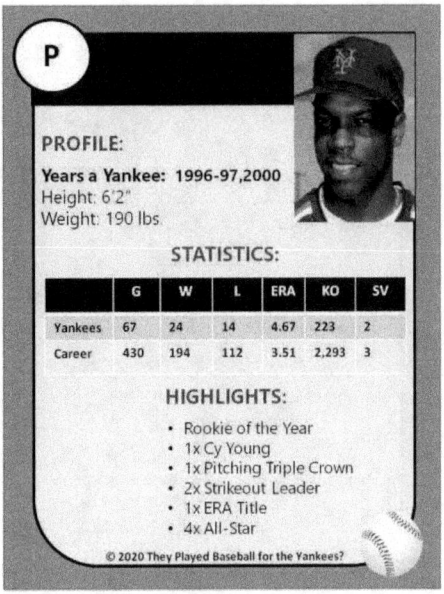

Twelve years later, at the age of 31, Gooden left the Mets and signed as a free agent with the cross-rival Yankees. After pitching poorly the first month of the 1996 season, Gooden was sent down to the minors. He soon returned with a shortened wind-up, and proceeded to no-hit the Seattle Mariners 2-0 on May 14, the first no-hitter by a Yankee right-hander since Don Larsen's perfect game in the 1956 World Series. Gooden ended the 1996 season at 11-7, his first winning record since 1991. After going 9-5 for the Yankees in 1997, he left the team, signing with the Cleveland Indians in 1998.

Gooden began the 2000 season with two sub-par stints with the Houston Astros and Tampa Bay Devil Rays, and was traded back to the Yankees mid-season. He would go on to have a respectable second stint with the Yankees, going 4-2 with a 3.36 earned run average as a spot starter and long reliever. He made one relief appearance in each of the first two rounds of the playoffs, but did not pitch in the 2000 World Series against his old team, the Mets.

After a difficult spring in 2001, 35 year-old Doc Gooden chose to retire rather than be released by the Yankees.

Frank Chance

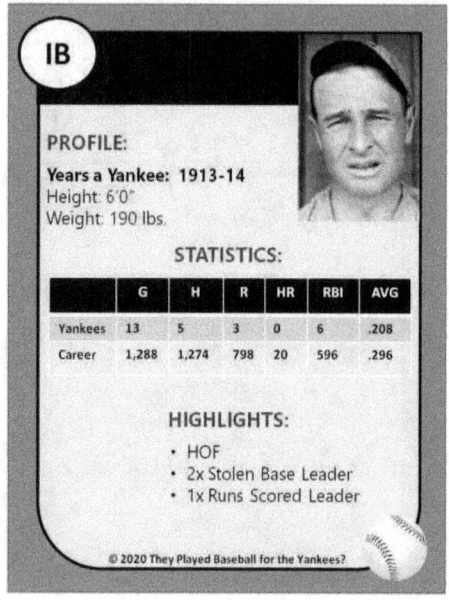

PROFILE:
Years a Yankee: 1913-14
Height: 6'0"
Weight: 190 lbs.

STATISTICS:

	G	H	R	HR	RBI	AVG
Yankees	13	5	3	0	6	.208
Career	1,288	1,274	798	20	596	.296

HIGHLIGHTS:
- HOF
- 2x Stolen Base Leader
- 1x Runs Scored Leader

© 2020 They Played Baseball for the Yankees?

Hall-of-Famer Frank Chance is probably best known for his association with fellow Chicago Cub infielders Joe Tinker and Johnny Evers. In 1910, the three of them formed what New York Evening Mail columnist Franklin Pierce Adams called the double-play trio of "Tinker-to-Evers-to-Chance".

In his 15 years with the Cubs, Chance hit .297 with 20 home runs and 590 RBIs. His best season was in 1903 when he recorded a .327 batting average and an at-the-time major league record 67 stolen bases. Chance was a player/manager from 1905 through 1910, leading the Cubs to four National League pennants and World Series championships in 1907 and 1908. In the 1910 World Series, Chance was ejected in game 3, becoming the first player ever ejected from a World Series game.

Chance had a tendency to crowd the plate, and was often hit in the head by pitched balls. Because of this, in 1912, Chance had multiple surgeries to correct blood clots in his brain. At the time, he was also unhappy with Cubs management - and they with him. As a result, Cubs owner Charles Murphy negotiated with the Yankees for Chance's release. In January 1913, Murphy released Chance while he was still recovering in the hospital.

Soon after, Chance signed a three-year contract with the Yankees as a player/manager. But, after playing in only 13 games the first two years of the contract, Chance left the Yankees before the 1915 season.

They Played Baseball for the Yankees?

Home Run Baker

John Franklin "Home Run" Baker played for the Philadelphia Athletics and New York Yankees during a time known as the "dead ball" era, where teams relied more on speed than power. From 1900 through 1919, stolen bases and hit-and-run type of "small ball" was the predominant strategy used during that time.

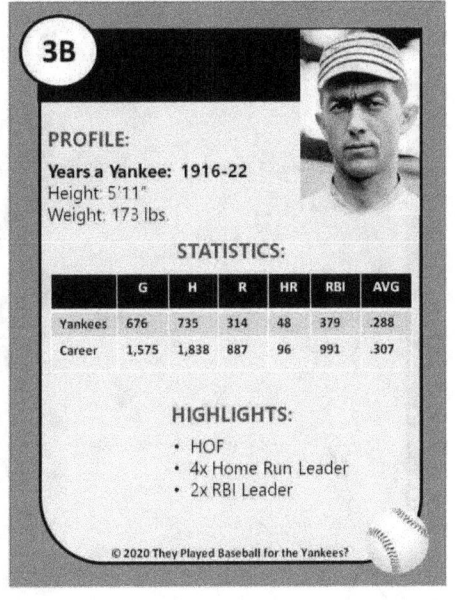

As a result of this style of play, the league leader in home runs had fewer than 10 round trippers 13 times between 1900 and 1920. The arrival of Babe Ruth in 1919 would change that forever, however.

Baker himself never hit more than a dozen home runs in a season, and only hit 93 homers in his 13-year career. Despite that, he led the American League in home runs from 1911 through 1914. As a result, he was often referred to as the "original home run king of the majors". His 130 RBIs in 1912 and 117 in 1913 also led the league.

After a contract dispute, the Athletics sold Baker to the Yankees in 1916 where he helped an anemic Yankees' offense for the next four years. Unfortunately, an outbreak of scarlet fever after the 1919 season would kill Baker's wife and infect his two infant daughters. Grief-stricken, and preoccupied with taking care of his daughters, Baker lost interested in baseball and sat out the 1920 season. However, when his daughters recovered, his desire to play returned, and Baker re-joined the Yankees in 1921. Baker appeared with the Yankees in the 1921 and 1922 World Series, before retiring at age 36.

They Played Baseball for the Yankees?

Jeff Reardon

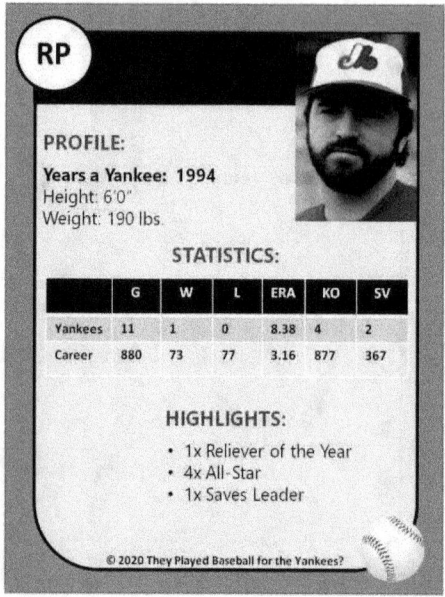

PROFILE:
Years a Yankee: 1994
Height: 6'0"
Weight: 190 lbs

STATISTICS:

	G	W	L	ERA	KO	SV
Yankees	11	1	0	8.38	4	2
Career	880	73	77	3.16	877	367

HIGHLIGHTS:
- 1x Reliever of the Year
- 4x All-Star
- 1x Saves Leader

© 2020 They Played Baseball for the Yankees?

After finishing the 1993 season with his highest earned run average since 1987 (4.09) and his fewest saves since 1981 (8), the Cincinnati Reds released 38 year-old Jeff Reardon after he spent two seasons being the set up man to closer Rob Dibble. A role Reardon was not used to, being a closer himself until joining the Reds. Just prior to spring training in February 1994, Reardon signed on with the Yankees.

Although he made the team and traveled with them, Reardon didn't perform well. After compiling an 8.38 earned run average and allowing 17 hits over 9 2/3 innings in 11 games, he retired from the Yankees, and Major League Baseball, on May 4, 1994.

At the conclusion of his 16-year career, Reardon stood second on the all-time saves list to Lee Smith, finishing with more saves (367) than walks (358). He actually briefly became Major League Baseball's all-time saves leader in 1992 when his 342nd save broke Rollie Fingers' previous record of 341, before Smith passed him in 1993. Reardon was the only reliever to have more than 20 saves every year from 1982 to 1988.

John Mayberry

Although John Mayberry played 15 years in the majors, it was his six years with the Kansas City Royals (1972-1976) where he really shined.

Considered one of the premier power hitters of his time, the left-handed slugger belted 22 or more home runs in five of the seasons, including a then team high 34 in 1975. The two-time All-Star drove in 100 runs or more three times, led the league in walks twice, and finished second in the Most Valuable Player voting in 1975.

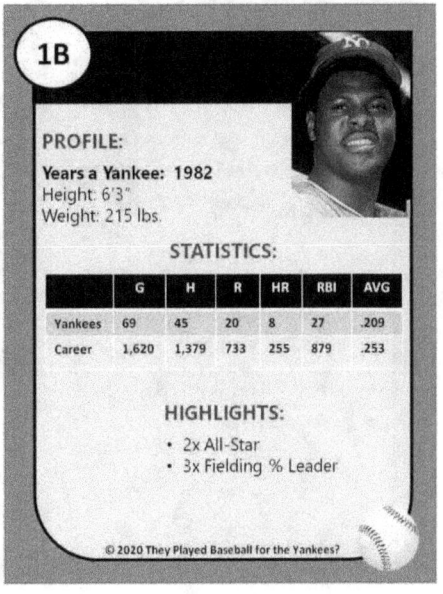

PROFILE:
Years a Yankee: 1982
Height: 6'3"
Weight: 215 lbs.

STATISTICS:

	G	H	R	HR	RBI	AVG
Yankees	69	45	20	8	27	.209
Career	1,620	1,379	733	255	879	.253

HIGHLIGHTS:
- 2x All-Star
- 3x Fielding % Leader

© 2020 They Played Baseball for the Yankees?

Mayberry was sold to the Toronto Blue Jays in 1978 following some off-field issues with the Royals during the 1977 playoffs which involved arriving late for games. After three years in Canada, including one where he hit 30 home runs, Mayberry was traded to the Yankees on May 5, 1982 after starting the season in Toronto. That year, in 69 games with the Yankees, Mayberry hit .209, although his playing time was reduced during August and September. Overall for the 1982 season, Mayberry batted .218 with 10 home runs and 30 RBIs. After finishing the season with the Yankees, he retired from baseball at the age of 33.

Upon his retirement, Mayberry held both the Royals and Blue Jays franchise records for most home runs in a single season (34 in 1975 with Kansas City; 30 in 1980 with Toronto). He played every inning of his major league career at first base, leading the American League three times in fielding percentage, while recording a .994 lifetime fielding percentage.

Johnny Mize

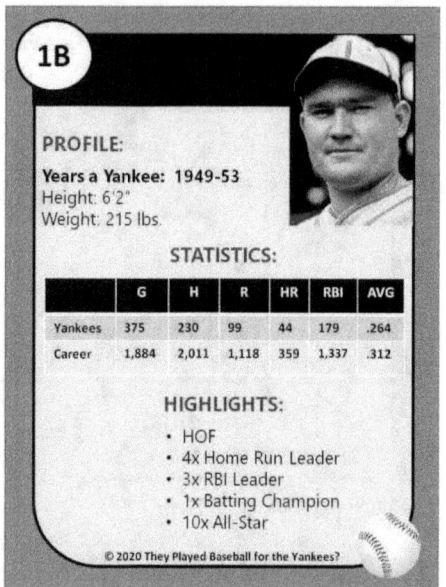

1B

PROFILE:
Years a Yankee: 1949-53
Height: 6'2"
Weight: 215 lbs.

STATISTICS:

	G	H	R	HR	RBI	AVG
Yankees	375	230	99	44	179	.264
Career	1,884	2,011	1,118	359	1,337	.312

HIGHLIGHTS:
- HOF
- 4x Home Run Leader
- 3x RBI Leader
- 1x Batting Champion
- 10x All-Star

© 2020 They Played Baseball for the Yankees?

"The Big Cat" began his Hall-of-Fame career in 1936 with the St. Louis Cardinals, and one year later hit .364 to finish second in the National League batting title race. Mize's 43 home runs in 1940 set a Cardinals team record that stood for nearly 60 years. At the end of the 1941 season, the 29 year-old Mize was traded to the San Francisco Giants where he played until 1949.

After spending 1943 through 1945 in the military, Mize returned and had the best year of his career in 1947 when he bashed 51 home runs and drove in 138 runs while hitting .302 for the Giants. In 1949, Mize, at 36 years of age and a part-time player now, was sold by the Giants to the Yankees for $40,000.

Mize spent the last five years of his career with the Yankees, mostly as a part-time player as well. "The Big Cat" became a member and valuable contributor to a team that won five consecutive World Series titles. In 1950, Mize hit 25 home runs to become the second player to have a 25-home run season in both leagues. In the 1952 World Series against the Brooklyn Dodgers, he hit three home runs and was robbed of a fourth by Dodger right fielder Carl Furillo.

In October 1953, at the age of 40, Mize announced his retirement, saying that he would rather retire while still popular with fans than to *"hang around until they start to boo"*. In his career, Mize won the Home Run title four times, RBI title three times, and one batting title.

Kevin Brown

From 1986 to 2005, Kevin Brown's signature sinker pitch helped him lead the American League in wins once, and top the National League in earned run average twice. He was also a six-time All-Star.

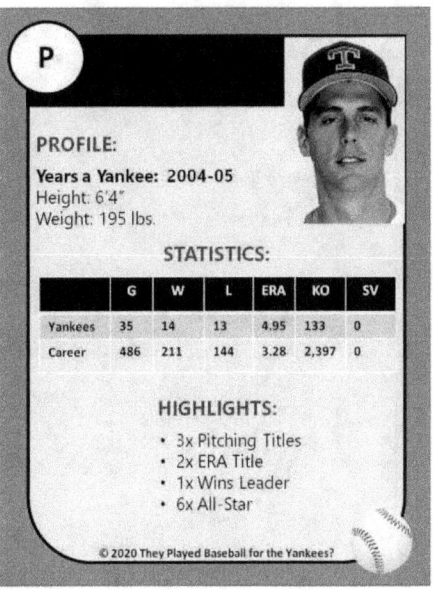

PROFILE:
Years a Yankee: 2004-05
Height: 6'4"
Weight: 195 lbs.

STATISTICS:

	G	W	L	ERA	KO	SV
Yankees	35	14	13	4.95	133	0
Career	486	211	144	3.28	2,397	0

HIGHLIGHTS:
- 3x Pitching Titles
- 2x ERA Title
- 1x Wins Leader
- 6x All-Star

© 2020 They Played Baseball for the Yankees?

Brown won a career-high 21 games with the Texas Rangers in 1992, and a World Series ring with the Florida Marlins in 1997. In 1999, Brown, a free agent five times in his career, signed a 7 year/$105 million contract with the Los Angeles Dodgers, becoming the first $100 million man in baseball.

On December 11, 2003, the Dodgers traded Brown to the Yankees in exchange for Jeff Weaver, Yhency Brazobán, Brandon Weeden, and $2.6 million dollars. The Yankees, of course, were obligated to fulfill the reminder of Brown's 7-year contract. In 2004, Brown experienced health problems resulting in a 10–6 record with a 4.09 earned run average, but not before winning his 200th career game on April 14. He pitched well in the Division Series that season, but lasted less than two innings in Game 7 of the 2004 American League Championship Series after giving up five earned runs.

Brown attempted a comeback with the Yankees in 2005, but missed several games during the season due to injury and finished the season at 4–7 with a 6.50 earned run average. On February 20, 2006, Brown announced his retirement at the age of 40.

Paul Waner

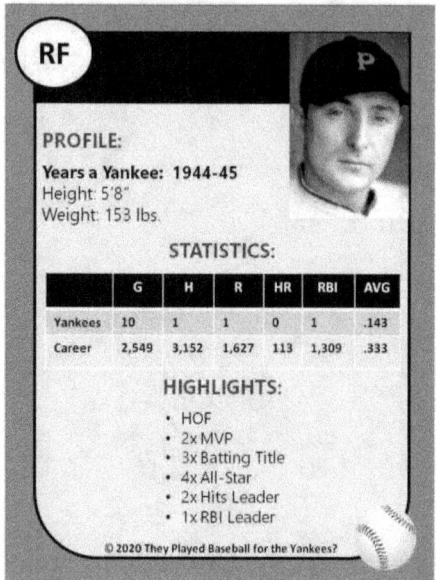

Paul "Big Poison" Waner played for four teams during a 20 year career between 1926 and 1945, most notably his first 15 seasons with the Pittsburgh Pirates. During that time, he led the National League in batting three times and was voted the National League's MVP in 1927.

Waner was the seventh player to accumulate over 3,000 hits in a career, collected 200 or more hits in eight different seasons, and had a lifetime batting average of .333. Waner also had one six-hit game, and five five-hit games.

Waner and his younger brother Lloyd hold the record for career hits by brothers with 5,611, outpacing the three Alou brothers (Felipe, Matty, and Jesús), and the three DiMaggio brothers (Joe, Dom, and Vince), who had 5,094 and 4,853 respectively.

After his 15-year stint with the Pirates, Waner played the next four seasons with the Boston Braves and Brooklyn Dodgers. On September 1, 1944, he was released by the last-place Dodgers and picked up by the Yankees the same day to provide the team a veteran bat off the bench during the final month of the season. Waner collected one hit in seven at-bats as the Yankees finished the year in third place.

In 1945, Waner began the season with the Yankees, pinch-hitting once and drawing a walk. On May 3, 1945, at the age of 42, he decided to retire.

They Played Baseball for the Yankees?

Other Players of Note

In the early days of baseball, up into the 1930's, seeing a colorful nickname attached to a player was a pretty common occurrence. For whatever the reason, these catchy nicknames began disappearing in the 1940's and were almost non-existent from the 1950's onward. But here are a few of the most noteworthy who played for the Yankees early in their history.

- Birdie Cree
- Boardwalk Brown
- Bobo Newsom
- Bots Nekola
- Braggo Roth
- Bubbles Hargrave
- Bullet Joe Bush
- Bump Hadley
- Chick Autry
- Chicken Hawks
- Cuddles Marshall
- Fenton Mole
- Frenchy Bordagaray
- Gabbie Street
- Ham Hyatt
- Hippo Vaughn
- Irish McIlveen
- Iron Davis
- Jumbo Brown
- Kemp Wicker
- Kiddo Davis
- Liz Funk
- Muddy Ruel
- Noodles Hahn
- Ping Bodie
- Rosey Ryan
- Roxy Walters
- Sad Sam Jones
- Shags Horan
- Slim Love
- Slow Joe Doyle
- Snake Wiltse
- Snuffy Stirnweiss
- Spec Shea
- Spud Chandler
- Truck Hannah
- Urban Shocker
- Yats Wuestling

The Yankees by the Numbers

The following shows where the Yankees franchise ranks among Major League Baseball teams in a variety of categories through the 2019 season, going back to 1903 when baseball in New York first began.

WINS

Rank	Team	Since	WINS
1	Giants	1883	11,165
2	Cubs	1876	10,982
3	Dodgers	1884	10,974
4	Cardinals	1882	10,918
5	Braves	1876	10,697
6	Reds	1882	10,599
7	Pirates	1882	10,545
8	Yankees	1903	10,378
9	Phillies	1883	9,825
10	Red Sox	1901	9,604

WINNING %

Rank	Team	Since	%
1	Yankees	1903	.570
2	Giants	1883	.535
3	Dodgers	1884	.528
4	Cardinals	1882	.520
5	Red Sox	1901	.519
6	Cubs	1876	.514
7	Indians	1901	.512
8	Reds	1882	.505
9	Tigers	1901	.504
10	Pirates	1882	.503

RUNS

Rank	Team	Since	RUNS
1	Cubs	1876	99,248
2	Giants	1883	97,268
3	Cardinals	1882	97,006
4	Braves	1876	95,747
5	Reds	1882	94,840
6	Pirates	1882	94,244
7	Dodgers	1884	93,875
8	Phillies	1883	92,749
9	Yankees	1903	89,040
10	Red Sox	1901	86,762

HOME RUNS

Rank	Team	Since	HRs
1	Yankees	1903	16,215
2	Giants	1883	14,682
3	Cubs	1876	14,375
4	Braves	1876	13,900
5	Tigers	1901	13,842
6	Red Sox	1901	13,712
7	Orioles	1901	13,518
8	Reds	1882	13,432
9	A's	1901	13,307
10	Phillies	1883	13,239

They Played Baseball for the Yankees?

BATTING AVERAGE

Rank	Team	Since	BA
1	Rockies	1993	.274
2	Red Sox	1901	.267
3	Yankees	1903	.266
4	Cardinals	1882	.266
5	Indians	1901	.266
6	Tigers	1901	.265
7	Giants	1883	.264
8	Pirates	1882	.264
9	Royals	1969	.264
10	Cubs	1876	.263

ERA

Rank	Team	Since	ERA
1	Dodgers	1884	3.53
2	Giants	1883	3.57
3	Yankees	1903	3.65
4	Braves	1876	3.66
5	Cardinals	1882	3.67
6	Cubs	1876	3.68
7	Pirates	1882	3.73
8	Reds	1882	3.75
9	Wh. Sox	1901	3.78
10	Mets	1962	3.79

WORLD CHAMPIONSHIPS

Rank	Team	Since	WS #
1	Yankees	1903	27
2	Cardinals	1882	11
3	Red Sox	1901	9
4	A's	1901	9
5	Giants	1883	8
6	Dodgers	1884	6
7	Pirates	1882	5
8	Reds	1882	5
9	Tigers	1901	4
10	Braves	1876	3

HALL OF FAMERS

Rank	Team	Since	HOF
1	Giants	1883	57
2	Braves	1876	53
3	Dodgers	1884	50
4	Cardinals	1882	47
5	Yankees	1903	46
6	Cubs	1876	45
7	A's	1901	41
8	Pirates	1882	40
9	Red Sox	1901	37
10	Reds	1882	36

Source: *"Baseball Reference"*: https://www.baseball-reference.com/

The Yankees – a Timeline

The following outlines some of the milestones of the New York Yankees beginning with their birth in 1903 as the New York Highlanders.

1900-1920

Jan. 9, 1903: Frank Farrell and Bill Devery purchase the defunct Baltimore franchise of the American League for $18,000 and then move the team to Manhattan.

Mar. 12, 1903: The New York franchise is approved as a member of the American League. The team will play in a hastily constructed, all-wood park at 168th Street and Broadway. Because the site is one of the highest spots in Manhattan, the club will be known as the "Highlanders" and their home field "Hilltop Park."

Apr. 22, 1903: The Highlanders play their first game, a 3-1 loss at Washington.

Apr. 23, 1903: The Highlanders record the first win in franchise history, a 7-2 decision at Washington. Harry Howell recorded the win.

Apr. 30, 1903: The Highlanders notch a 6-2 win vs. Washington in their inaugural home opener at Hilltop Park.

Apr. 11, 1912: Pinstripes first appear on Highlanders' uniforms, creating a look that would become the most famous uniform design in sports.

April, 1913: The Highlanders are officially renamed the "Yankees" after moving to the Polo Grounds, home of the National League's New York Giants.

Jan. 29, 1915: Col. Jacob Ruppert and Col. Tillinghast L'Hommedieu Huston purchase the Yankees for $1.25 million.

Apr. 24, 1917: George Mogridge becomes the first Yankee to throw a no-hitter in a 2-1 win at Fenway Park.

1921- 1940

Jan. 3, 1920: The Yankees purchase the contract of Babe Ruth from the Boston Red Sox for $125,000 and a $350,000 loan against the mortgage on Fenway Park.

September, 1921: The Yankees clinch their first AL pennant.

May 5, 1922: Construction begins on Yankee Stadium.

May 21, 1922: Col. Ruppert buys out Col. Huston for $1.5 million.

Apr. 18, 1923: Yankee Stadium opens with a 4-1 win over the Boston Red Sox before a reported crowd of 74,200. Babe Ruth hits the Stadium's first home run.

June 1, 1925: Lou Gehrig begins his streak of 2,130 consecutive games played, pinch-hitting for Pee Wee Wanniger.

Sept. 30, 1927: Babe Ruth breaks his own Major-League record with his 60th home run on the season's final day.

Apr. 16, 1929: The Yankees become the first team to make numbers a permanent part of the uniform (numbers would become standard for all teams by 1932).

June 3, 1932: Lou Gehrig becomes the first player to hit four home runs in a single game in the Yankees' 20-13 win at Philadelphia. He remains the only Yankee to hit four home runs in one game (as of 2019).

They Played Baseball for the Yankees?

July 14, 1934: Babe Ruth hits the 700th home run of his career off Tommy Bridges in the second inning of a 4-2 Yankees' win at Detroit's Navin Field.

Nov. 21, 1934: The Yankees purchase Joe DiMaggio from the San Francisco Seals of the Pacific Coast League for $50,000.

May 2, 1939: Lou Gehrig's playing streak of 2,130 consecutive games ends when he does not make an appearance in a 22-2 Yankees' win at Detroit. Babe Dahlgren plays first base for the Yankees and contributes a double and a home run.

July 4, 1939: "Lou Gehrig Appreciation Day" is held at Yankee Stadium. His uniform number (4) is the first to be retired in Major League Baseball and Gehrig makes his famous *"Today I consider myself the luckiest man on the face of the earth"* speech.

1941- 1960

May 15, 1941: Joe DiMaggio's 56-game hitting streak begins with a single off Edgar Smith in a 13-1 loss vs. Chicago at Yankee Stadium.

June 2, 1941: Lou Gehrig dies of Amyotrophic Lateral Sclerosis at the age of 37.

July 17, 1941: Joe DiMaggio's consecutive-game hitting streak ends at 56 when he goes 0-for-3 in a 4-3 Yankees' win at Cleveland. Indians' third baseman Ken Keltner twice robs DiMaggio of hits with great fielding plays. DiMaggio then hits in the next 16 straight games to give him hits in 72 of 73 games.

May 28, 1946: The first night game is played at Yankee Stadium and the Yankees suffer a 2-1 loss to Washington before 49,917 fans.

Apr. 27, 1947: "Babe Ruth Day" is celebrated throughout Major League Baseball.

They Played Baseball for the Yankees?

June 13, 1948: Babe Ruth's uniform number (3) is retired at Yankee Stadium's 25th Anniversary celebration. The Babe makes his final Stadium appearance.

Aug 16, 1948: Babe Ruth dies in New York of throat cancer at age 53.

Apr. 17, 1951: Mickey Mantle makes his Major-League debut, going 1-for-4 in a 4-0 win over Boston at Yankee Stadium.

Sept. 28, 1951: In Game One of doubleheader vs. Boston at Yankee Stadium, Allie Reynolds tosses his second no-hitter of the season (he had previously no-hit the Indians at Municipal Stadium in Cleveland on July 12).

Dec. 12, 1951: Joe DiMaggio officially announces his retirement.

Apr. 17, 1953: Exactly two years after his Yankee debut, Mickey Mantle hits what is recognized as the game's first "tape-measure" home run, a 565-foot clout off the Senators' Chuck Stobbs at Washington's Griffith Stadium.

Oct. 5, 1953: The Yankees win a record fifth consecutive World Championship.

Oct. 8, 1956: Don Larsen hurls the only perfect game in World Series history, a 2-0 win over Brooklyn in Game Five at Yankee Stadium.

1961- 1980

Oct. 1, 1961: Roger Maris hits his 61st home run in the season's final game to establish a Major-League record.

June 24, 1962: Jack Reed's two-run, 22nd-inning home run ends the longest game in Yankee history, a 9-7 win at Detroit.

Nov. 2, 1964: CBS purchases 80% of the Yankees for $11,200,000. The network later buys the remaining 20%.

June 8, 1969: "Mickey Mantle Day" is celebrated at Yankee Stadium and his uniform number (7) is retired.

Aug. 8, 1972: The Yankees sign a 30-year lease to play in a remodeled Yankee Stadium to be completed in 1976.

Jan. 3, 1973: A limited partnership, headed by George M. Steinbrenner III as its managing general partner, purchases the Yankees from CBS.

Apr. 6, 1974: The Yankees begin the first of two seasons at Shea Stadium, playing the first home game outside Yankee Stadium since 1922. The Yankees accumulate a 90-69 record overall at Shea.

Dec. 31, 1974: Free agent Catfish Hunter signs a then-record five-year contract.

Aug. 1, 1975: Billy Martin replaces Bill Virdon for his first of five stints as manager.

Apr. 15, 1976: Remodeled Yankee Stadium opens with an 11-4 win over Minnesota Twins. The Twins' Dan Ford hits the first home run.

Oct. 14, 1976: Chris Chambliss' ninth-inning home run off Mark Littell in Game Five of the ALCS vs. Kansas City gives the Yankees their 30th pennant.

Nov. 29, 1976: Free agent Reggie Jackson signs a five-year contract.

Oct. 18, 1977: Reggie Jackson hits three home runs in Game Six of the World Series vs. the Los Angeles Dodgers at Yankee Stadium.

June 16, 1978: Ron Guidry establishes a franchise record by striking out 18 batters in the Yankees' 4-0 win vs. California at Yankee Stadium.

They Played Baseball for the Yankees?

Oct. 2, 1978: The Yankees, 14 games behind Boston at one point, defeat the Red Sox, 5-4, at Fenway Park in only the second playoff game in AL history. Bucky Dent's homer over the Green Monster completed the comeback, clinching the pennant for the Pinstripes.

Aug. 2, 1979: Yankees Captain Thurman Munson dies in a plane crash in Canton, Ohio, at age 32 (his number "15" is immediately retired).

Dec. 15, 1980: Free agent Dave Winfield signs a then-record 10-year contract.

1981- 2000

July 24, 1983: The Yankees and Kansas City play the infamous "Pine Tar" game at Yankee Stadium as George Brett hits a two-out, ninth-inning home run off Goose Gossage to give the Royals an apparent 5-4 lead. The umpires nullify the homer because the pine tar on Brett's bat is above the allowable 18 inches and Brett is called out for using an illegal bat. The Yankees win 4-3.

Aug. 18, 1983: Kansas City's protest is upheld and the "Pine Tar" game concludes with the Royals winning 5-4. When play is resumed, Yankee pitcher Ron Guidry is in center field for the final out of the top of the ninth while left-handed first baseman Don Mattingly is at second. Royals' reliever Dan Quisenberry retires the Yankees in order in the bottom of the ninth.

Apr. 28, 1985: Billy Martin is named manager for the fourth time, replacing Yogi Berra.

Dec. 14, 1985: Roger Maris dies at age 51 in Houston, Texas.

July 18, 1987: Don Mattingly homers off Texas' Jose Guzman to tie Dale Long's Major-League record of hitting a home run in eight consecutive games (Mattingly hits 10 home runs during the streak).

Sept. 29, 1987: Don Mattingly hits a grand slam off Boston's Bruce Hurst, setting a Major-League record with six grand slams in a season.

June 23, 1987: Billy Martin is replaced as manager of the Yankees for the fifth and final time. Lou Piniella is named manager for the second time.

Dec. 25, 1989: Billy Martin dies in an automobile accident at age 61.

Aug. 14, 1993: "Reggie Jackson Day," his uniform number (44) is retired.

Sept. 4, 1993: Jim Abbott pitches a 4-0, no-hit win over the Indians at Yankee Stadium.

Aug. 13, 1995: Mickey Mantle dies of cancer at age 63 in Dallas, Texas.

Sept. 6, 1995: Lou Gehrig's major league record of 2,130 consecutive games played is broken when Baltimore's Cal Ripken, Jr. plays in his 2,131st.

May 14, 1996: Dwight Gooden hurls only the eighth regular-season no-hitter in Yankee history, a 2-0 blanking of the Seattle Mariners at Yankee Stadium.

June 16, 1996: Mel Allen, the legendary "Voice of the Yankees" from 1939-64, dies at age 83 in Greenwich, Connecticut.

Oct. 26, 1996: The championship trophy returned to the Bronx after the Yankees defeat Greg Maddux and the Braves in Game 6 of the World Series for their 23rd title.

May 17, 1998: David Wells tosses only the 14th regular-season perfect game in baseball history, the first ever by a Yankee.

They Played Baseball for the Yankees?

Sept. 25, 1998: The Yankees establish an American-League record with their 112th win of the season after a 6-1 victory vs. Tampa Bay at Yankee Stadium, breaking the mark of 111 by the 1954 Cleveland Indians. They complete the season with an AL record 114th victory on September 27 vs. Tampa Bay.

Oct. 21, 1998: The Yankees complete an incredible season with a four-game sweep of the San Diego Padres in the World Series to capture the franchise's 24th World Championship. Their 3-0 win gives the club a season record of 125-50 (114-48 in the regular season, 11-2 in postseason).

Mar. 8, 1999: Joe DiMaggio dies at age 84 in Hollywood, Florida.

July 18, 1999: On "Yogi Berra Day," David Cone tosses only the 15th regular-season perfect game in baseball history one season after David Wells accomplishes the feat. Coincidentally, Don Larsen-- who tossed a perfect game in the 1956 World Series--throws out the ceremonial first pitch.

Sept. 9, 1999: Jim "Catfish" Hunter dies at age 53 in Hertford, North Carolina.

Oct. 27, 1999: The Yankees play Baseball's last game of the century and complete a four-game sweep of the Atlanta Braves to capture their 25th World Championship. The 4-1 win is also the club's 12th straight in World-Series play, tying the record of the 1927, 1928 and 1932 Yankees.

Oct. 26, 2000: Yankees win their 26th World Championship in five games against the New York Mets. It was the first "Subway Series" since 1956.

2001- 2020

Nov. 4, 2001: In one of the most exciting editions of the World Series, the Diamondbacks beat the Yankees in seven games. Luis

Gonzalez lined a Series-winning single off Mariano Rivera in the ninth inning of Game 7.

Dec. 13, 2001: Jason Giambi, the runner-up in the AL MVP balloting, signs a seven-year contract with the Yankees.

June 13, 2003: Roger Clemens became the first pitcher since Nolan Ryan in 1990 to reach the 300 win mark. The Rocket also joined another fraternity that night at Yankee Stadium, striking out the 4,000th batter of his career. Only Ryan (5,714) and Steve Carlton (4,136) have more strikeouts than Clemens.

April 11 & 14, 2004: Mike Mussina and Kevin Brown record their 200th victories in back-to-back games, becoming the first teammates in major league history to do so.

Sept. 30, 2004: Bernie Williams launches a walk-off home run against the Twins at Yankee Stadium, clinching the Yankees' seventh consecutive American League East crown, as New York advanced to the playoffs for a 10th consecutive season.

Jan. 11, 2005: The trade to bring Randy Johnson to New York becomes official.

Oct. 1, 2005: In the 161st game of the season, the Yankees defeat the Red Sox at Fenway Park to clinch their eighth consecutive AL East crown.

May 14 - June 1, 2009: The Yankees set an all-time major league mark with 18 consecutive errorless games, safely handling 660 chances over the stretch.

Sept. 11, 2009: Derek Jeter breaks Lou Gehrig's all-time franchise mark of 2,721 hits with a single off Baltimore's Chris Tillman at Yankee Stadium.

They Played Baseball for the Yankees?

Oct. 4, 2009: Alex Rodriguez hits a three-run home run and a grand slam in the sixth-inning of the season finale at Tampa Bay, setting an all-time AL mark with seven RBIs in an inning.

Nov. 4, 2009: The Yankees win their 27th World Championship, defeating Philadelphia in Game 6 of the World Series, 7-3.

July 9, 2011: Derek Jeter becomes the first Yankee to collect 3,000 career hits with a home run off of Tampa Bay's David Price. Jeter would finish with 3,465 hits in his career.

Aug. 25, 2011: The Yankees became the first team in history to hit three grand slams in a game.

Sept. 19, 2011: Mariano Rivera set the new major league record for career saves with his 602nd.

June 19, 2015: Alex Rodriguez records his 3,000th career hit on June 19 with a home run off the Tigers' Justin Verlander.

Oct. 1, 2015: The Yankees become the first AL club to reach 10,000 victories, a win that clinched a playoff berth.

Aug. 12, 2016: Alex Rodriguez hit just nine homers before playing his final game on August 12, leaving him with 696 for his career, fourth all-time.

Source: https://www.mlb.com/yankees/history

Book Sources

- "*Baseball Almanac*": https://www.baseball-almanac.com/
- "*Baseball Reference*": https://www.baseball-reference.com/
- "*Retro Sheet*": https://www.retrosheet.org
- "*Society for American Baseball Research*": https://sabr.org/

Author's Bio

Jeff Wagner is a native of the Bay Area in California, and has been a fan of Major League Baseball for over 50 years.

Jeff is a fan of all Bay Area sport teams, including the San Jose Sharks and Golden State Warriors, as well as teams from both the San Francisco and Oakland sides of the bay: San Francisco 49ers/Giants and the Oakland Raiders/A's, making him a dying breed as this is almost unheard of today in the Bay Area! Jeff has written several blogs on his experiences:

- Our Bay Area teams have been very good to us:
  http://drummerjeff.blogspot.com/2012/10/our-bay-area-sport-teams-have-been-very.html
- My Top 10 Favorite Moments in Bay Area Sports History:
  https://drummerjeff.blogspot.com/2019/04/my-top-10-favorite-moments-in-bay-area.html
- My Top 10 Toughest Moments in Bay Area Sports History:
  https://drummerjeff.blogspot.com/2019/04/my-top-10-toughest-moments-in-bay-area.html

Jeff also likes playing the drums, and enjoys a blessed life with his wife Amy and their Pug Celia.

Other Books Written by Jeff:

They Played Baseball for the Giants?
ISBN-10: 1481931865
ISBN-13: 978-1481931861

Pug Shots: The Many Faces of a Chinese Pug:
ISBN-10: 1481931865
ISBN-13: 978-1481931861

www.ingramcontent.com/pod-product-compliance
Lightning Source LLC
LaVergne TN
LVHW051511070426
835507LV00022B/3057